George Stella's Livin' Low Carb

Family Recipes Stella Style

George Stella

SIMON & SCHUSTER PAPERBACKS

NEW YORK • LONDON • TORONTO • SYDNEY

SIMON & SCHUSTER PAPERBACKS
Rockefeller Center
1230 Avenue of the Americas
New York, NY 10020

First Simon & Schuster paperback edition 2005

SIMON & SCHUSTER PAPERBACKS and colophon
are registered trademarks of Simon & Schuster, Inc.

For information about special discounts for bulk purchases,
please contact Simon & Schuster Special Sales at
1-800-456-6798 or business@simonandschuster.com

Please consult your physician before starting this
or any other diet, exercise, or lifestyle change program.

Designed by Charles Kreloff

Manufactured in the United States of America

10 9 8

Library of Congress Cataloging-in-Publication Data
Stella, George.
    [Livin' low carb]
    George Stella's livin' low carb : family recipes Stella style. /
George Stella.—1st Simon & Schuster pbk. ed.
      p.   cm.
    Includes index.
    1. Low-carbohydrate diet—Recipes. I. Title: George Stella's
Livin' low carb. II. Title: Livin' low carb. III. Title.

RM237.73.S746   2005
641.5'6383—dc22   2004058978

ISBN-13: 978-0-7432-6997-1
ISBN-10:   0-7432-6997-7

I DEDICATE THIS BOOK, AS I DO MY ENTIRE LIFE,
TO MY BEAUTIFUL WIFE, RACHEL.
I LOVE YOU NOW MORE THAN EVER,
AND FOREVER MORE.

GEORGE

Acknowledgments

Without the continued support of my wife, Rachel, and my sons, Anthony and Christian, I would not have been around to write this book. No man could hope for a more loving, caring family.

I also wish to thank my late mother and father. I pray they know how grateful I am to them for who I am. My mother, Veldyne, was a great cook. She inspired me at an early age and taught me that I could do anything I put my heart into. My father, George, was a vaudeville entertainer and ragtime piano player—it's his fault I'm such a big ham!

Thanks also to my sisters and their husbands, Virginia and Skip Olson and Stephanie and Johnny Miles. They were always there for us—even when they had nothing themselves. I thank God that I now have the opportunity to return the favor.

Loving thanks to my in-laws, Claire and Ernest Barrette, who have been a constant source of strength and support for Rachel and me throughout our marriage. I love them very much and always have.

I'd also like to thank Dr. Frank Campisi. He took me under his wing from the day we met, literally giving me the clothes off his back and the shoes off his feet. He helped me get back to work when I first got out of the wheelchair. He will always be a valued friend.

Our heartfelt thanks as well to our very special friends Dr. Tim O'Leary and his lovely wife, Kathleen. They have been our benefactors, friends, and confidants. They blindly believed in us and helped us when we were at our lowest. I believe they were heaven-sent; without them none of this would have been possible.

I would also like to give special thanks to my new friends, Maria Conti and Cory Williamson. Maria is my manager and has her hands full trying to keep me in line! Her husband, Cory, helped me write this book. We also want to thank their cool kids, John and Zoe, for graciously sharing their parents with us so we could get this book completed in time.

Thanks also to Susan Barry, my literary agent, for handling all the business stuff that would have made my head spin right off my shoulders!

Thanks to Melissa Possick as well, who was the first person in the publishing world to contact us—after seeing us featured on an episode of *48 Hours* on CBS—and who brought us to Simon & Schuster. There, in the capable hands of our editor, Amanda Murray, the idea of this book became a reality.

Many "red-lined" thanks to our working editor, Betsy Rapoport. She needed the patience of a saint to put up with Cory and me!

I'd also like to thank the photographer, Mark Thomas, the prop stylist, Nancy Micklin Thomas, and the food stylist, Anne Disrude.

These acknowledgments would not be complete if I did not thank my new family at Food Network. I love them all, but Jeanne Shanahan will always have a special place in my heart. Jeanne championed me at Food Network when everyone else was treating me like a low-carb stalker. I also want to thank Bob Tuschman of Food Network. He shared my belief that we could help and inspire people with a low-carb show and translated his faith into action with *Low Carb and Lovin' It*.

Finally, I will always be eternally indebted to the late, great Dr. Atkins, for providing me the key to success—low-carb!

Thanks again to all of you for helping to start us on a journey you usually only read about in books!

Contents

George Stella's Livin' Low Carb

Stella Style

I'm George Stella, the Low-Carb Chef, and six years ago I weighed 467 pounds. That's right, **467 pounds**! I was only thirty-nine years old, but I was suffering from congestive heart failure and living on disability. I couldn't even button the largest pair of pants I could find at the department store, so I used a safety pin instead and let my shirts hang down in front so no one could see. By then, it didn't really matter anyway. I could hardly walk, so I stayed home in a wheelchair most of the time. I couldn't even make it across the kitchen without stopping for a breather.

Only a few years earlier I'd been a chef at some of the finest restaurants in Florida—Café Max, Sausalito Restaurant, Windows on the Green, the list goes on and on. Somehow, though, I lost control of my life. I began to eat, and then to eat even more, and when it was all over, I'd eaten my way out of a life most chefs only dream of.

I was born in Bridgeport, Connecticut, in 1959. I was kind of a chubby kid, but not what you'd really call overweight. When I was eleven years old, my father, a former vaudeville entertainer who had fallen on hard times, decided to move the family to Florida. Times were tough, but the weather sure was an improvement. After a few years of sweating under the hot Florida sun, I'd pretty much burned my baby fat off. It wasn't until I experienced heart problems as a teenager that I had my first real problems with my weight. The treatment I was given—massive doses of the steroid prednisone—actually ended up causing a lot of my problems, including gaining a lot of weight. Luckily for me, my mother found a doctor who understood what was really going on—just before I was about to undergo heart surgery! With his help, I was able to wean myself off the steroids and bring my weight down again.

By then I had already been cooking for years. I got my start early, thanks to a good friend from the neighborhood, Jimi Volpe. At the time he was working as a line cook at the Ranch House Restaurant on Deerfield Beach, right next to the pier. He was only fifteen and had lied about his age in order to get the job. I was only fourteen, but I was tired of pushing a rusty old lawn mower around to make money. So I followed Jimi's advice, told the manager I was sixteen, and before long I had my first job in a restaurant—washing dishes!

I didn't wash dishes for long, but I was in the kitchen for good! Jimi kept pestering the manager to let him teach me how to cook the line, and finally the manager gave in. I had found my calling, and from that moment I decided that I wasn't just going to learn how to cook—I was going to become a chef!

There was just something about cooking that clicked for me right from the beginning. I just loved working in the kitchen. I loved being in the middle of all the action, surrounded by the noise and the smells of the cooking food. I loved learning from everybody I worked with too. I was hooked on cooking, but I got hooked on some pretty bad eating habits too. That's where all my problems started.

The results of those bad habits wouldn't show up for a while though, and once I got past my heart problems, my luck changed for the better. I met my wife, Rachel, and we got married and had children. With a family to provide for, I really had to concentrate on my career, and it wasn't long before all those hours in a restaurant kitchen, and my terrible eating habits, began to take their toll. I still remember the first time—after stopping the steroids—that my weight climbed back above 200 pounds. I wasn't happy about it, but I wasn't too worried either. I'm drawing the line here, I told myself. All it would take was a little willpower.

Well, it turned out willpower wasn't enough. By the time I turned twenty-five, I weighed more than 300 pounds, and by the end of the year I was in the hospital again—after suffering a massive heart attack!

They kept me in the hospital for a couple weeks until my condition stabilized. While I was there, I lost over thirty pounds, and I remember thinking that I could just keep going if I put my mind to it. Plus the cardiologist was lecturing me every day about losing weight, and I had a family to support. When I left the hospital I was really determined to regain control of my eating—and my life!

For another few years, I succeeded. The problem was that every time my weight went up and down, it seemed to go up a little more and down a little less. I was working at bigger and better restaurants, but I kept having to buy bigger and bigger pants too! I knew I had a problem—a big problem—but I just couldn't face up to it.

I told myself that all the great chefs were big. I remember the first time I saw Paul Prudhomme, the famous New Orleans chef who brought Cajun cooking into the mainstream. I thought to myself that as least I wasn't as big as he was. (It wasn't long, though, before I was.) In the meantime, I kept telling myself that a skinny chef just wouldn't look right. If his food was any good, how could he be so skinny?

It was then that I became the executive chef at the Phillips Petroleum Company's showcase restaurant, Windows on the Green. All the while, though, my health was failing. You'd think I'd have learned my lesson after the first heart attack, but I just kept eating myself sick, even though I'd had a long history of heart trouble. Each extra pound just made things worse. My back began to act up, and then my knees and my feet started bothering me too.

By the time I was thirty, my weight was affecting both my health and my career. Suffering from chest pains and shortness of breath, I started missing work. That didn't do much for my career. Each time I changed jobs, I promised myself I'd finally figure out a way to lose weight, but I just didn't know how to do it.

It was a miracle my heart didn't just give out—for a whole bunch of reasons. Finally one of my doctors told me that if I didn't start losing weight right away I'd never see my next

1997

birthday. I'll never forget the way he leaned across his desk and looked into my eyes as he said it. I can still hear those words today. But even a sentence of death wasn't enough to make me change. I'd been wrapping myself in a protective blanket of food for so long that as soon as I wheeled myself out of his office all I wanted to do was get back home and eat some more. I was scared, and I was worried, but I just couldn't stop eating. I'd been doing everything the wrong way for so long that I didn't believe I could change.

In the years that followed that visit to the doctor's office, not only didn't I lose weight, I actually put more weight on. By that time, I could no longer find clothes that fit me. I couldn't ride on buses or on airplanes. In fact, there were cars I couldn't get into. And, because I couldn't stay on my feet for more than a few minutes at a time, I could no longer work. Towards the end, I left the house for only one reason—to eat! (In other words, I only left the house for the same reason I was

1995

stuck in the house!) Besides, I knew what I looked like, and I was tired of hearing people make fun of me whenever I went. And just carrying that extra weight made everything so much harder. It was like carrying another man on my back—and a big man too.

Finally, when my weight climbed so high that it kept me from working at all, I just gave up. I was on disability by then and basically just stayed home. I was really, really depressed. I'd really loved working in the kitchen. I had loved dreaming up new recipes and seeing them end up on the menu. That was the strangest part of it all. My work in the kitchen made other people very happy, but it made me and my family miserable.

I finally hit bottom in 1998. My father, who was still going strong in his nineties, died suddenly in Michigan. I was at my heaviest, and in poor health. I'd been out of work so long, that even if I'd been able to fit into an airline seat, I couldn't have afforded to go to his funeral. He was buried on my thirty-ninth birthday, and I couldn't be there.

How did it happen? How could someone with so much to live for almost eat himself to death? I didn't understand it myself, and everybody else had just one question for me.

"Why don't you just stop eating so much?"

Well, believe it or not, not eating was one of my biggest problems. That's right, **not eating was one of my biggest problems**! Go ahead and ask any chef how many meals he eats during a twelve- to eighteen-hour shift in a hot kitchen. I'll bet I know what the answer will be every time: not one! Sure, you pick here and there, but the truth is there's no time to eat. Plus, food just doesn't cut it once you're running on caffeine and adrenaline. I'd start every morning with a cup of coffee, then drink another cup on the way to work. As soon as I got to the restaurant, I'd make myself some more—you guessed it—coffee! By the time I felt like eating, we were deep into our prep work, and I couldn't take the time. And that, of course, was nothing compared to how crazy things got once the first customers arrived—it was off to the races!

Of course I did eat, but I ate the worst sort of food at the worst time of the day. I'd get home every night around midnight, drop my keys on the table, and go right to the refrigerator. Hungry and dehydrated, I'd start by drinking a couple quarts of juice (or, in other words, corn syrup, dye, and water). Then I'd really get to work. I'd eat whatever leftovers I could find, then grab myself a big bag of chips, and follow it all up with ice cream. Once I got started, I couldn't stop, especially after starving myself all day. I ate anything I could get my hands on: cookies, candy, cake, pizza, soda, crackers, pastries—it didn't matter to me.

The result was that everything I ate was stored as fat. To understand this, it helps if you think of your body as a furnace. If you keep your body's furnace going all day, it'll burn everything you throw into it and provide you with plenty of energy. By not eating, you let the fire go out; if you throw another log on, it won't burn—it'll just smoke! It's the same thing with eating. If you don't eat, your body's furnace cools down, and nothing you eat afterwards will burn—it'll just get stored as fat! And if the food you eat is heavy in carbohydrates—well, you're bound to get into trouble sooner or later.

I wasn't the only one in the family with a weight problem.

When I first met Rachel, she was so slender and full of life and energy that she was about the last person in the world you'd think would ever have a weight problem. She was even working in a commercial bakery, but nothing stuck to her ribs.

Twenty years and two kids later, she was carrying around seventy-five unnecessary pounds. Like most people who gain weight, she hadn't put it all on at once. She gained eighty-five pounds when she had Anthony, but she'd lost almost all the weight by the time Christian came along three years later. While pregnant with him, she was a little better about watching what she ate, so she only put on about fifty-five pounds. Those were the pounds, though, that she just couldn't seem to take off afterwards.

She did lose some weight right after Christian was born, and given what we know now, it seems pretty clear why. Our oldest son, Anthony, was really hyper as a little boy. After trying everything else, Rachel finally cut all the sugar out of his diet—and I mean all of it! And guess what? Her plan worked! Anthony quieted down, and to her surprise, **she** lost weight! (In just a couple of months, she went from a size 14 to a size 12.) It didn't last long though. As he got older, Anthony got easier to deal with, Rachel slowly started allowing sugar back into the house again, and before she knew it, she was back up to a size 16. Finally, she just gave up trying. This is how she put it, in her own words.

> I'd just gotten sick and tired of trying to lose weight all the time. It never worked—all it did was make me feel worse. So one day I asked myself, why am I even bothering? I'm fat already. In fact, everybody in the family's fat, so we might as well just all be fat together.

From then on, she started eating whatever she wanted to and let all of us do the same. It's not surprising that we all continued to gain weight, especially if you listen to what Rachel was bringing home from the supermarket in those days.

> Grocery shopping back then was all about how I could get the most amount of food for the least amount of money, and I didn't really care what kind of food it was. So to start with, I loaded the cart up with chips, pretzels, cookies, ice cream, and single-serving iced cakes. I also bought a lot of macaroni and cheese, mostly because it was Christian's favorite, but also because I thought it was good for him! I bought lots of regular pasta and big jars of store-bought spaghetti sauce. Every single time I went to the store I always bought big packages of hot dogs and, of course, hot dog buns to go with them. I bought boxes and boxes of sugary cereal and lots of potato salad too, you know, from the deli counter.
>
> My favorite snack food in those days was cheddar cheese popcorn, and I always bought that in the big "Smart Bag." I also bought huge containers of

powdered coffee creamer, the biggest bottles of ketchup I could find, and those gigantic tubs of margarine (which we went though almost as fast as ice cream)! I never bought name brands—just store brands or generic stuff.

Bananas were our favorite fruit, except when oranges were in season. Then we ate them morning, noon, and night. I mean we were living in Florida, and we always knew someone who couldn't get rid of all of theirs, so we'd get them for free. I always made room in the cart for two or three gallons of fruit drink too. You know, the kind that costs practically nothing because all it really is is just colored corn syrup. Of course, I didn't know that then, or if I did, I didn't care.

Anyway, I always bought chicken, and ground beef too, but only whatever was on sale. I mostly bought frozen vegetables, because the fresh ones always seemed to be more expensive. In the summer months we did buy a lot of corn on the cob, but once again, only because it was always on sale. Our favorite vegetable by far was frozen French fries. I could never buy enough of them, the way George and the boys went through them. I bought gallons of milk too, and the cheapest white bread I could find. Of course, now I know that's the least nutritious kind, but back then I didn't know any better. And to go with the bread I bought the biggest jars of store-brand peanut butter and jelly I could find. Plus, I always bought lots of candy. That was my real downfall. I couldn't wait for the holidays back then, because the day after everything was half off. So I just scooped it up by the armful, especially after Halloween and Easter.

It's pretty easy to see why Rachel had trouble losing weight, but her problem was nothing compared to those of our kids, especially Christian.

Christian weighed 300 pounds by the time he was fifteen. He was normal sized at birth, but by the time he went to kindergarten he was pretty chunky, and he just kept getting bigger and bigger every year. For him, every day started with sugar. He'd eat sweetened cereal, or doughnuts, or waffles, or pancakes just soaked in cheap syrup. Between meals he snacked on crackers, chips, pretzels, and candy. For dinner, in addition to whatever else was being served, he always loaded his plate with either pasta or potatoes.

As a result, he got heavier and heavier. You can imagine how the other kids treated him. He was bullied and teased and picked on from the moment he set foot in school. (He always told us that he wasn't, but we knew it couldn't be true. He finally admitted just how bad it was during an interview on a Food Network special in early 2004.)

I'm not surprised he kept it to himself. He was so ashamed of the way he looked back then that in the photographs we've got of him, he's always holding one of his hands up in front of the camera lens—and holding something to eat in the other. As Rachel put it, by then we'd just given up. We were fat, and we weren't going to get any skinnier. Our point of view got so twisted that when our older son, Anthony, shot up to 225 pounds, none of us even thought of him as overweight. He just had a "little gut."

What could I say? I had gotten so big that the fronts of all my shirts began to wear through from the steering wheel rubbing against my stomach while I drove. I could barely walk—forget about cooking the line. And then there were the things people said.

At first it was only little children, but gradually I began to hear adults whispering behind my back as well. By the time I went over 400 pounds, they didn't even bother to whisper. It was as if I wasn't a person anymore, just some dumb animal that couldn't understand anything.

I still remember the last flight I took (before I took the weight off). The stewardess took one look at me, dug out a seatbelt extension, then loudly enough for everybody on the plane to hear it, said: "Take this. You're going to need it."

I was so embarrassed I wanted to disappear, but of course that's the one thing you can't do when you weigh over 400 pounds. But that wasn't what hurt the most. I was dragging my family down with me, and I knew it.

One day, Anthony's girlfriend—who had gone on a diet herself so she could fit into her prom dress—left a beat-up paperback book on our kitchen table. That book was *Dr. Atkins New Diet Revolution.*

A couple days went by before Rachel sat down at the kitchen table, picked up the book, and started leafing through it. I was sitting in my wheelchair in the living room, half asleep in front of the TV. Before long, I could hear her laughing in the kitchen. After a while, my curiosity got the better of me, and I called out and asked her what was so funny? Rachel started reading parts of the book aloud to me, and before long we were both laughing.

Who did he think he was kidding with this stuff? According to his book, it was suddenly all right to eat the foods everybody had been telling us **not** to eat—foods like red meat, butter, cheese, and bacon. How could you eat food like that and lose weight? It was obviously a crock. Still, reading about all that mouthwatering food made us hungry, so we decided to give it a try—you know, just for laughs. We didn't believe for a minute it would work, but what did we have to lose?

To be honest with you, we never actually even read Dr. Atkin's book. There were way too many tables and graphs—and it was just too long. But we did leaf through the front of the book, and we got the idea pretty quickly. As Dr. Atkins put it, our bodies weren't designed to deal with all the high-carbohydrate, low-nutrition foods we were shoveling into them. The healthiest diet, he said, was one high in protein and fat, and super-low in carbs.

When we looked at what we ate during a normal day, it sure began to make sense. It seemed like we didn't eat anything **but** carbs from the time we got up in the morning to the time we went to bed. So we decided to give the Atkins Diet a try.

It wasn't easy at first. We had to say goodbye to a lot of our favorite foods—bread and pasta topped the list—but at least we could go back to using butter again and eating things like bacon. We became serious label readers too, and tried to cut as many carbs as we could out of our lives. Before we knew it, the pounds began to fall off.

To tell you the truth, even today it's hard to believe that low-carb worked so well for us, especially when we remember how we laughed at the idea in the beginning. While we've taken the low-carb ball and run with it in another direction, the truth is that without Dr. Atkins's help you wouldn't be reading this book today. He was, to put it simply, a great man. While the medical establishment was ignoring his work, and the U.S. government was all but calling him a quack, he continued to spread the good word about eating low-carb. His basic idea—that the modern diet of the world's most industrialized countries consists of overprocessed, carbohydrate-heavy, sugar-laden junk—is now widely acknowledged to be the truth.

To be honest, though, right from the beginning there were parts of the Atkins Diet that we just couldn't stomach. The first was giving up coffee. It may seem kind of silly to make such a big deal out of it, especially given all the weight I had to lose, but drinking coffee was really important to me. (And don't even try serving me decaf or a cup of coffee without half-and-half!)

Serving sizes were a big problem too. Atkins insisted on portion control, but some part of me rebelled against the idea that I couldn't have as much as I wanted. (I know that sounds crazy, because I was so desperate to lose weight, but that's how I felt.)

Rachel and I knew that there was no way we could stick with low-carb if we couldn't eat as much as we wanted. Starving ourselves had never worked. If the problem was **what** we were eating—not how **much** we were eating—then why couldn't we eat as much "good food" as we wanted? So right from the beginning we just let ourselves have as much as we wanted—as long as it was low-carb—and just ignored the advice about portion control. More than any other reason, I think we succeeded in losing weight because we never felt deprived. (We may have been counting carbs, but we could always tell ourselves that we weren't on a diet!) The point is that when we sat down to eat, we knew we wouldn't have to get up before we were satisfied—**and so we looked forward to eating**! Over time, as our bodies adjusted to life without massive daily doses of carbohydrates, we found ourselves eating less and less.

The other problem we had with Atkins, right from the beginning, was that it was just too boring. Almost as soon as we started, Rachel and I began trying to broaden the menu. The recipes just weren't exciting enough, especially when it came to fruits and vegetables. All in all, there were just too many No's on the Atkins plan, and we didn't want to go through the rest of our lives without so many of our favorite foods. What's life without pizza or lasagna? Who wants to watch a movie without something to munch on, or watch a football game without some kind of chips? What do you mean no pumpkin pie at Thanksgiving? And don't even try to get between me and a slice of cheesecake!

Finally, we didn't like the idea of buying prepackaged mixes (which showed up in a lot of the Atkins recipes). While there's nothing wrong with buying ready-made low-carb products, as chefs it rubbed us the wrong way. The question was this: How could we eat low-carb and still enjoy our favorite foods? To answer that question, Rachel and I went to the one room in the house where we'd always done our best thinking—the kitchen. There we returned to what we'd been doing for more than twenty-five years—that is, inventing new recipes. And while we were at it, we invented a whole new way of eating. We call it *Stella Style!*

What's *Stella Style*?

Stella Style means eating fresh foods, using low-carb ingredients to reinvent your old favorites, and developing better eating habits. It means eating low-carb meals, snacks, and desserts that are quick, easy to make, and that use simple ingredients you can find in your local grocery store. Most of all, Stella Style means eating food you like and not worrying about how much you eat!

Stella Style means putting food first. As a veteran of restaurant kitchens, I firmly believe that food is meant to be enjoyed. If you don't like what you're eating, you're going to be bored and unhappy, and people who are bored and unhappy with what they're eating quickly go back to their old eating habits. You don't have to say goodbye to all your favorite foods—you can recreate them *Stella Style!* All you have to do is use your imagination.

Once Rachel and I made up our minds to create a new style of eating, we kept at it. It took us many years and lots of trial and error to come up with the perfect *Stella Style* **New York Ricotta Cheesecake**, but now it's one of our most-requested recipes. (You'll find it on page 216.) We experimented with several dozen different recipes for pizza crusts before settling on one that was just right for our **Low-Carb Pizza**—one that didn't use refined flour and yet satisfied our craving for this favorite snack (see page 58).

Don't get us wrong. We've certainly tried the low-carb alternatives that are available at the grocery stores, but we always felt ourselves coming back to our roots as chefs, bakers, and "professional" food lovers. We vastly prefer homemade alternatives; they're cheaper, they don't have preservatives, and because you make them yourself, you know exactly what you're getting. When you crave the taste of chocolate—and trust me, I often do—just check out my recipes for **Chocolate Pecan Bon Bons**, **Chocolate Pecan Brownies**, or **Chocolate Ganache**! I'd rather make it *Stella Style* than buy something at the store. All it takes is a few simple ingredients, a few minutes to prepare, and I feel better eating it because I know what's in it!

Holiday foods were our biggest creative challenge, but we figured out a way to have our **Praline Pumpkin Pie**—and eat it too (along with the **Traditional Oven-Roasted Turkey**, **Garlic Mock Mashed Potatoes**, and all the other trimmings of real Thanksgiving feast). Hey, I admit it—we had a lot of recipe failures before we found the keepers—but we stuck with it anyway. Where there's a Stella will there's a

Stella way! It wasn't too long before the whole family got into the act—shopping, cooking, and inventing recipes *Stella Style*. What did we have to lose?

I'll tell you what we had to lose—**560 pounds**!

That's right, as a family in just two years we lost more than **560 pounds**! I went from 470 pounds to 210 pounds—and I'm not done yet! Rachel went from 205 pounds to 130 pounds. Christian dropped from 300 to 140 pounds, and Anthony went from 225 to 160 pounds.

Think about it: 560 pounds is more than most families of four weigh to start with! And what's more, we've kept the weight off for years.

Once we started eating *Stella Style* we never looked back. As the pounds melted away, we decided to spread the word. In 2001, Rachel and I started our own company, The Low-Carb Chefs, and designed a special program called the "Complete Low-Carb Home Chef Program" to help support those interested in living low-carb. We traveled all around Florida teaching people how to carb-proof their pantries (as we'll explain below), shop low-carb, and cook gourmet low-carb meals. We even went on an Atkins Cruise—not as customers, but as gourmet chefs—to teach passengers how to bring this delicious lifestyle home with them. We also began talking about *Stella Style* more and more on television, and in magazines.

2004

In early 2004, I hosted *The Low-Carb Revolution*, a Food Network special about living low-carb. Then in May of the same year, Rachel and I launched our very own show on the Food Network: *Low Carb and Lovin' It*. Every week we share the secrets of *Stella Style*—and some of our favorite recipes—with millions of viewers.

The response to our show has been overwhelming! We get tons of letters and e-mails from viewers all across the country, and most of them say the same thing—we want more! More *Stella Style* recipes, that is. Hey, we're happy to oblige!

Why Does Eating *Stella Style* Work?

The last thing I want to do is load you down with lots of technical information (if you're like me, you just want to eat, not go back to school), but I will share a few of the basics so you'll understand why eating *Stella Style* works so well.

Your body gets all the energy it needs from the calories in fat, protein, and carbohydrates. When it wants energy, it burns those calories. The easiest calories to burn come from carbohydrates, so that's what your body turns to first when it's searching for fuel.

Our own government recommends that the average person consume 300 grams of carbohydrates a day! This means that when your body's looking for something to use to make energy, it turns to those easy-to-burn carbs first, leaving that harder-to-burn fat right where you don't want it—around your middle. A carb-heavy diet actually makes you hungrier and increases your cravings, so you keep eating, and that spare tire around your waist just gets bigger and bigger. That's why even if you count calories, or watch your portion size, when you're eating a lot of carbs you just keep getting bigger—and hungrier!

So what do I mean when I say "low-carb"? Just like it sounds, a low-carb diet means you really cut back on the carbs. Instead of eating the government-recommended 300 grams of carbohydrates a day, you have somewhere between 20 and 60, depending on your own metabolism and how close you are to your desired weight. Once you start eating low-carb, you'll quickly find out what works best for you. Everyone's different. My point is that you don't need to get all caught up with numbers when you eat *Stella Style*. In fact, when you eat low-carb *Stella Style*, you don't need to count carbs. Ever. If you follow the guidelines in this book and learn to make these recipes, you'll eat until you feel satisfied, without ever having to worry about how much food is on your plate. You'll be eating fewer carbs a day so that your body will start to burn fat instead of carbohydrates for energy—and that's when the unwanted pounds will start to melt away.

Sure, in order for low-carb to work you've got to cut back on some foods and avoid others. You've got to break your dependence on high-carbohydrate processed foods, and that includes breads, cereals, crackers, chips, pastas, sugary sodas and juices, desserts packed with sugar, and certain fruits and vegetables. But that doesn't mean your meals have to put you to sleep!

How Does *Stella Style* Differ From The Atkins Diet?

The biggest difference between **Stella Style** and Atkins is that I think about eating from the perspective of a chef, not a doctor. It always seemed kind of funny to me that so many of the low-carb cookbooks out there were written by doctors. It's not that I have something against doctors—in fact, if it weren't for two or three really good doctors, I wouldn't be here today. But if you wouldn't have your tonsils taken out in a kitchen, why would you use recipes that come out of a doctor's office? **Stella Style is about getting you out of the doctor's office and back into the kitchen where you belong!**

This is a cookbook, not a science book! Sure, we're here to tell you how we broke our dependence on high-carb junk, and lost weight doing it, but don't look for any chapters about the science of low-carb here. You can find that information in any one of a hundred places on the Internet, or in your library, or in a bookstore. I want you to keep this book in your kitchen, not in your office!

Think about it this way. Have you ever bought a computer, opened the 200-page manual, and after trying and failing to finish *even one chapter,* just gone ahead and put the computer together without it? I don't know about you, but I use my computer all the time, and I never read the manual!

The point is you don't need a book full of tables to learn how to lead a low-carb lifestyle. It's just not as complicated, or as boring, as some people make it out to be.

You won't find any menus, tables, or items to check off in this book. Who needs them? You don't use salt and pepper to add up the bill when you eat out, do you? Then why would you need a calculator to eat?

If you want to know how many carbs are in a particular food, especially if you want to make substitutions of your own, check out one of the many carbohydrate counters available in bookstores or on the web. My goal is to get you to forget about counting carbs, or calories, or portion size. Still, I understand as well as anyone that it might take a while for you to get used to eating *Stella Style*. So I've included the net carbohydrates per serving of every recipe in this book so you can get a feel for how low-carb these recipes really are. But you don't need any other guideline beyond these simple rules: Eat when you're hungry, and stop when you're satisfied. What could be simpler?

You're plenty smart enough to make your own, informed decisions about what you eat. Besides, we're not proposing anything new—most of mankind has been living a low-carb lifestyle for *tens of thousands of years*. Simply put, low carb is about *fresh food*. You don't need a Ph.D. in science to understand that. **Just eat fresh foods**! It's that simple! And when you have to shop for foods with a longer shelf life, **read the labels**! That's the only way you can keep products with added sugars—which, as I'll explain, hide behind all sorts of different names—as well as hydrogenated oils and "trans" fats (the "bad" fats)—out of your shopping cart and off your pantry shelves. Everything you need to know is right there on the side of the box or the can (although I'll bet the manufacturers of all that high-carbohydrate junk wish it weren't). And watch out for low-fat foods that are just packed with sugar!

Finally, before we move on to the information you'll need to get started, I have one more thing to say. I wrote this book because eating low-carb literally saved my life, but I can't make that decision for you. If you want to start living a low-carb lifestyle, talk to your doctor and get the go-ahead first. If you decide to give it a try, just remember that I'm here to support you by sharing the story of what living low-carb has done for my family and me.

Getting Ready for
Stella Style

The first thing you've got to do before starting **Stella Style** is learn how to **carb-proof your pantry**. (If you'd been living in Florida three or four years ago, Rachel and I could have done this for you, because it was one of the many services we provided when we first began working as the *Low-Carb Chefs*. Now, I'm afraid you're going to have to do it yourselves.)

The good news is that it couldn't be simpler. Just start at one end of the pantry, start filling boxes with all the high-carbohydrate foods you've been eating for years, and take them to your local food bank. How do you know what to keep and what to toss? Just read the labels. Here are the basic rules.

Rule #1: Get Rid of the Hidden Sugar and Bring in Sugar Substitutes

The first thing to go is all that stuff that's filled with sugar—high in carbohydrates, low in good nutrition. Of course, this means getting rid of that bag of sugar, but don't stop there because you'll find sugar in a ton of foods. The hardest part of finding the sugar is that manufacturers don't always call it "sugar" on the label. You'll find sugar hiding behind dozens of different names. I can't even list them all here, but watch out for: sugar, syrup, corn syrup, HFCS (or high-fructose corn syrup), fructose, maltose, dextrose, and sucrose. You'll also want to keep natural sugar sources such as brown sugar, honey, molasses, and maple syrup, off your shelves, at least until you reach your maintenance weight.

Once you start reading labels, you're going to be pretty surprised to find out where all that sugar's been hiding. Sure, you expect to find it in candy, and in cakes and pies, and sugary children's cereals. But once you start looking, you'll find it in ketchup and other tomato products, condiments, salad dressings, deli meats—even in vanilla extract! Take all of that stuff out of your pantry and fridge right now. You're going to substitute products that say "**no sugar added**" right on the label. (But even here, you've got to be careful. You'll find plenty of chocolate recipes in this cookbook, but make sure you use unsweetened chocolate and cocoa powder—**not** "no-sugar-added" cocoa mix!)

Meat, poultry, fish, and shellfish are naturally low in carbs, and they're a big part of eating *Stella Style*. However, if you buy deli meats, you'll have to ask the people behind the counter to give you only "no-sugar-added" sliced turkey and the like. And watch out for hot dogs, bologna, and other meat products; they can be chock full of fillers that are high in carbs. Read the labels!

Go through your pantry and fridge and get rid of those drinks filled with sugar. Instead fill those shelves with diet soda (the kind that has no calories, not the kind that boasts "half the calories," since it's filled with carbs). And don't forget Crystal Light, seltzer (plain or flavored), and club soda too.

Did you know that sugar hides in beer and wine too? Even the new low-carb beers are higher in carbs than dry white and red wine, while hard liquor is totally carb-free. However, keep reading those labels. Dark rum, for example, almost always has added sugars. And keep this in mind too: Alcohol is a fuel for your body, just like fat and carbohydrates, so if you're drinking a lot, your body won't burn as much fat.

Once you've tossed out the sugar in your pantry, on your refrigerator shelves, and in all the cans, bottles, and boxes where it's been hiding, bring in our favorite sugar substitute, Splenda. For baking, you'll need a measure-for-measure sugar substitute to get the right proportions in the recipe. If using any other sugar substitutes, follow the directions on the package, keeping in mind that you cannot cook with most other substitutes. Again, Rachel and I have found that Splenda does the best job in any recipe that involves heating or baking.

Rule #2: Low-Fat Is Not Your Friend

If you're like Rachel and me, you probably thought that filling your fridge and pantry with low-fat foods would help you lose weight. Wrong! All those "low-fat" foods in the fridge are packed with sugar, and are therefore high in carbohydrates! Get rid of 'em! Don't cheat here because the hardest part of changing the way you eat is keeping the wrong foods out of reach. Think about it. The cravings you've developed over the years are not going to disappear overnight. Until you re-educate your body, you just have to stay away from the junk.

From now on, your refrigerator is going to have **only full-fat dairy products**. And while you're poking around in the fridge, don't worry about eggs; they're definitely included in *Stella Style*.

Rule #3: "Diet" Doesn't Always Mean "Low-Carb"

Have you stashed a bag of diet candy on your shelf to ease those cravings? Uh oh—go read the label. Most diet candy, like a lot of diet foods, is high in carbs. Toss it. But don't worry, I won't make you give up your sweets, you'll learn to make them yourselves in a very few minutes—*Stella Style!*

Rule #4: Watch Out for Bad Fats

Certain fats are great for *Stella Style*. In general, you want stuff that's high in monounsaturated fats and oils. When you cook *Stella Style*, you'll use canola oil, peanut oil, and olive oil for most recipes. You want to stay away from hydrogenated oils and "trans" fats. The good news is these are easy to avoid when you're eating *Stella Style*, because you won't find these in fresh foods, just in overprocessed ones.

Rule #5: Out with the White Flour

Eating *Stella Style* means getting rid of all the highly processed, overrefined white flour products that are probably a big part of your diet. That means saying goodbye to the white flour on your shelf, as well as everything made from it: bread, pasta, crackers, pretzels, snack chips, cereal, cakes, pies, muffins, and mixes of all kinds. (Whole wheat flour is allowed during maintenance.)

Rice and potatoes are also extremely high in carbs, so you won't find them lurking in any of my recipes. Hunt them down in your pantry, as well as all the foods made out of them, like potato chips, rice cereals, snacks, and so forth.

You may be feeling a little panicky by now. Don't worry! I promise you that you won't miss these high-carb foods once you're eating **Old-Fashioned Egg Mock Potato Salad**, **Deep-Fried Onion Rings**, and **Sausage and Herb Stuffing**!

Remember, Rachel was a professional baker. So even though I'm asking you to toss out your white flour, I'd never ask you to do without muffins, pizza, and our own mock pasta! You'll find recipes for them all here! Just bring in the soy flour (which you should keep in the fridge or freezer), and the wheat or oat bran, and you'll be ready for a whole new world of baking!

Rule #6: Choose the Right Fruits and Veggies

Fresh fruits and vegetables are a huge part of eating *Stella Style,* and I'd never ask you to give them up. However, some fruits and vegetables are naturally so high in carbs that I don't include them in my recipes. Here's a brief list below. It's not complete, so check out a carbohydrate counter if you're not sure.

OUT	IN
Carrots	Fresh herbs
corn	broccoli
potatoes	cauliflower
peas	cabbage
navy beans	cucumber
black beans	celery
lima beans	lettuce
bananas	zucchini
apricots	pumpkin
oranges	squash
pears	summer squash
plums	spaghetti squash
prunes	radishes
papayas	bean sprouts
watermelon	snow peas

OUT	IN
grapes	spinach
mangoes	collard greens
	mushrooms
	garlic
	onions (in moderation)
	green onions (scallions)
	leeks
	peppers
	asparagus
	eggplant
	tomatoes (in moderation)
	green beans
	jicama
	avocado
	honeydew melon
	cantaloupe
	strawberries
	blueberries
	blackberries
	raspberries
	lemons and limes (in moderation)

I love fresh fruits and vegetables because they're higher in nutrition than canned products (which can also be full of salt or other additives you don't need). So keep plenty of the right fruits and veggies on hand!

Rule #7: Think Alternatives

Stella Style doesn't mean doing without, it means finding creative ways to reinvent the foods you love. The key is keeping the right stuff on hand, so you can whip up a *Stella Style* recipe whenever—or long before—the next craving strikes! Here are just a few examples of creative substitutions or alternates you can use in place of your old high-carb favorites.

High-Carb	Alternate
sugar, candy	sugar substitute
chocolate	unsweetened baking chocolate, cocoa powder
soda and juice	diet soda, Crystal Light, seltzer, club soda, water (plain and fizzy), tea, coffee
refined (white) flour	soy flour (keep refrigerated or in the freezer), and wheat and oat bran
bread, cereal, crackers, potato chips, pretzels	beef jerky
salad dressings (with sugar)	olive oil, canola oil, vinegars
peanut butter (with sugar)	macadamia, pecans, walnuts (in moderation), sunflower seeds, almonds, and hazelnuts
canned soup	sugar-free beef and chicken bouillon
baking extracts	sugar-free baking extracts
ketchup (with added sugars)	salsa (no added sugars)
low-fat or skim dairy products	whole-milk dairy products

Of course, this list isn't meant to be complete; it just covers the basics. Remember, if you have any doubts about which foods should go and which foods can stay, **just read the labels!**

Grocery Shopping *Stella Style*

The next thing you've got to do for **Stella Style** is to change the way you shop for food. The answer, you'll be happy to hear, is simple: **Shop the outer aisles of the supermarket!** That's almost all there is to it. Just grab a cart and work your way around the exterior walls of the store. That's where you'll find the strawberries, blueberries, and raspberries, the cantaloupe and honeydew melon. That's where you'll find the broccoli and cauliflower, the spinach and mushrooms, and all the wonderful varieties of lettuce. That's where you'll find the fresh dairy aisle, with cartons of whole milk and heavy cream, and the whole-milk cheeses like Cheddar, provolone, mozzarella, ricotta, and cream cheese. That's where you'll find the beef, chicken, turkey, pork, and fish. That's where you'll find the frozen foods, too, and lots of them are low-carb! **Just read the labels!** That's also where you'll find the cold cuts (don't forget to look for "no sugar added") and in the supermarkets that sell them the dry red and white wines.

If you stick to the outer aisles, there's really only one place you have to stay alert, and that's the fresh produce and fruit aisle. You'll definitely want to push your cart past the fruits and vegetables listed as OUT on page 19–20. Other than that, all you really have to remember are these three things: **Shop the outer aisles, read the labels, and check your handy carb counter if you have any questions!**

Eating Out

Of course, you're not always going to eat at home, so even if you've carb-proofed your house and started shopping the outer aisles, you still need to think about what you're going to order when you eat out.

One of the most frequently asked questions we get on our Internet message board is this: Did you change the restaurants you went to once you started low-carbing? The answer—and it's a big surprise to most people—is NO! We ate at exactly the same restaurants we used to—we just ordered differently. Restaurants with buffets, for instance, were one of our favorite places to eat, and believe me, even though we were low-carbing, we still kept going! All we did was switch the kinds of food we ate.

In the old days, we loved buffets because you never had to wait to be served, and for someone who's always hungry, that's a big advantage. (Plus you could hide how much you were eating.) We used to load up on the bread, and rolls, and potatoes, to say nothing of the desserts, but once we began low-carbing we just started at a different place in the serving line. We ate lobster, prime rib, grilled fish, and clams or mussels. There was always turkey, too, and ham, and rotisserie chicken. There were roasts, chicken wings, and spareribs—to say nothing of the salad bar, which was almost all low-carb. The truth is that we were already eating a lot of low-carb foods, but we put so much high-carb foods on top of them that it didn't matter. So all we had to do was avoid the things that had gotten us into so much trouble in the first place. We stayed away from the desserts and didn't even go near the pasta, rice, or potatoes. The funny thing is that after a few weeks went by, we didn't go back as often for refills. Once our metabolisms began to change, we just didn't need as much food to feel full.

The truth is, as our carbohydrate cravings slowly faded away, we started eating at home more and more. Sure, we still go out from time to time (who doesn't want a break every once in a while?) but the truth is that our house is so full of good food— a lot of it already prepared, frozen, and ready to eat—that it's often easier for us to eat at home than it is to go out! Here's another way to look at it. Now we go out to eat only when we want to, not because there's nothing in the fridge that interests us!

Cooking Ahead

Cooking ahead is another critical part of *Stella Style*. Try doubling or tripling your favorite recipes and then freezing the leftovers! You'll never know how many times, especially during the first few months we were low-carbing, we were saved by being able to reach into the freezer and pull out some **Turkey Vegetable Soup**, or **Meat Lasagna**, or best of all, a low-carb dessert like **Neapolitan Parfaits** or **Chocolate Ganache**! You know what you like to eat, and with just a little help, you can fill your pantry, refrigerator, and freezer with low-carb meals and snacks that will keep your cravings under control.

Start by making a list of all the foods your family likes, especially proteins and veggies. Proteins should be from all sources, not just red meats. Chicken, fish, seafood, pork—they're all fair game! As for vegetables, sooooo many of them are allowed on low-carb, but you just don't hear about them! In fact, way more are allowed than aren't! Broccoli, spinach, mushrooms, spaghetti squash, lettuce, celery, cauliflower, eggplant, zucchini, and garlic are all *Stella Style* vegetables, as well as tomatoes and onions in moderation.

After listing all the foods your family really likes, identify the ones that are naturally low in carbs, and then try and reinvent the ones you just can't do without! For instance, you can add Cheddar cheese or chopped veggies to a meat loaf instead of bread crumbs, or "bread" pork chops with seasoned soy flour. You can use sugar substitutes, whipped cream, soy flour, and unsweetened chocolate to recreate your favorite desserts. You can use cauliflower to create mock mashed potatoes and spaghetti squash as a substitute for pasta. We'll go into this in more detail in the recipes themselves, but for now, just remember this: There's almost always a way to reinvent your favorite foods *Stella Style*, using a little imagination and some low-carb ingredients from your supermarket or health food store.

Finally, before we go on to the recipes, there's just one more thing to cover. Some of the recipes that follow require special equipment (always included at the bottom of the list of ingredients). Most of the equipment really isn't that special at all (like six-cup muffin tins, springform pans, grill pans, and outdoor grills); you've probably already got them on hand. Feel free to use nonstick cookware and bakeware, even if not specifically called for, in place of ordinary muffin tins and baking sheets. When cooking *Stella Style*, just use your head and feel free to substitute food or equipment whenever and wherever it makes sense.

Stella Style: A Lifestyle, Not a Diet

Once you get going, I'll bet you're going to be surprised at how easy it is to stick to this new way of eating! Remember, *Stella Style* isn't a diet. It's a lifestyle—a lifestyle devoted to healthy, satisfying eating habits and good food! And, once you get started, you'll be surprised at how quickly everyone else wants to join in too.

Our son Christian is a perfect example. When Rachel and I made the switch to low-carb, we never once thought about trying to force it on him. (By this time, Anthony was grown up and living on his own, so we didn't put any pressure on him either.) Anyway, for those of you out there who have teenagers, you know they'll never accept anything you try to force down their throats. Worse still, if you tell them something's good for them, you might as well forget about it! So even though we let *him* decide what he wanted to eat—or maybe *because* we let him decide—Christian eventually started picking at all the low-carb foods on the table, and before you know it, he was hooked. He just couldn't stay away from all that delicious food!

Then again, who would turn down a sizzling slice of **Low-Carb Pizza**, just dripping with cheese and pepperoni? Or a plate of **Anaheim Shrimp Scampi** sautéed in olive oil and garlic? Or a big helping of *Stella Style* **New York Ricotta Cheesecake**, with only six net carbs? Does that sound like a diet to you? And trust me, I'm just getting started.

2004

Maybe you'd prefer a crisp **Key West Caesar Salad** (topped off with your choice of shrimp, sirloin, chicken, or salmon). Or perhaps you're in the mood for garden-fresh **Grilled Summer Vegetables**. Or how about a plate of **Tequila Chicken** (one of my all-time favorites)? And don't forget all the low-carb, high-protein foods that you've been warned to avoid for years—foods like **butter, eggs, and bacon**. You can eat them all to your heart's content when you're low-carbing *Stella Style*.

If you're anything like me, your mouth is starting to water right now, and that's the whole point! *Stella Style* is all about the food! If you feel *obligated* to eat certain foods, instead of being able to eat the foods you really want, before long you'll go back to eating the way you used to—the way that made you reach for this book in the first place! Once again, all you've got to do is **learn how to make the right food**

choices, reinvent your favorite recipes using low-carb ingredients, and develop healthier eating habits. Never forget, when you're low-carbing *Stella Style*, you don't have to quit eating until you're full.

It almost sounds too good to be true, doesn't it? Well, just remember this—we did it. We **did** what all the others are **just talking about**! My family and I lost hundreds of pounds and, what's more, we've kept the weight off for years! So just start turning the pages and learn how to do it yourself—*Stella Style*!

Morning Starters

There is no meal more important than breakfast! Why? Because if you're eating *Stella Style,* you've got to **eat to lose weight**, and that means making breakfast an "unbreakable" part of your morning routine.

One of the reasons *Stella Style* works so well is that you don't have to scrimp on your portions. You can eat until you're satisfied—as long as you're making the right food choices. So not only is there no reason to skip meals, you'll actually make it *harder* to lose weight by not eating! Why? Because your body's metabolism works just like a furnace; if you let the fire go out, nothing you put into your stomach afterwards will burn. Therefore, you've got to get into the habit of making yourself a delicious *Stella Style* breakfast every morning.

The good news is that our **Morning Starter** recipes are sooo good, sooo easy to make, and sooo satisfying, that once you get into the habit, you'll never want to skip breakfast again! After all, who doesn't want to sit down to a stack of delicious **Blueberry Pancakes** just smothered in real butter? Or maybe you'd prefer an omelet stuffed with cheese, peppers, and ham? Or a couple of **Rachel's Raspberry Muffins**? The point is there's plenty to choose from, and a lot of the recipes you'll find here can be made ahead of time and then kept handy in the freezer or refrigerator.

Most people skip breakfast because they're always running late in the morning. They just don't have time to prepare anything. But that's no excuse if you're living a low-carb lifestyle. Breakfast is so important that you have to learn to make time for it. Even if it takes setting your alarm clock ten or fifteen minutes ahead, you've got to do it. Trust me, it'll be worth it once you bite into a warm slice of my **Kitchen Sink Quiche**! And just try to imagine the looks on your kids' faces when they find a platter of Rachel's **Chocolate Chip Muffins** waiting for them on the kitchen table. (If that sounds too much like candy for breakfast, keep in mind that there's more sugar in one bowl of cereal than in a whole plate of Rachel's muffins!) Finally, don't forget that *Stella Style* means combining meals, and mixing and matching. So don't forget to look through the fridge before deciding what to eat. Maybe you'll find a couple slices of ham you can drop into the skillet with your eggs.

Anyway, whatever low-carb food you choose, **don't skip breakfast!** You need to start a fire in your body's furnace every morning, so that your body will burn whatever you eat more efficiently during the day. Don't skip meals when you're eating *Stella Style,* and don't forget to snack either. **You've got to eat to lose weight**, and that means eating morning, noon, and night. For now, though, let's turn our attention to the following collection of delicious, easy-to-make **Morning Starters**—*Stella Style!*

Blueberry Pancakes

Blueberry pancakes are a great way to start your day, but that doesn't mean they're only for breakfast. They're also great for brunch, or any time at all!

Vegetable oil cooking spray or butter
2 large eggs
⅓ cup heavy cream
¼ cup water
1 teaspoon sugar-free vanilla extract
½ cup soy flour
2 tablespoons sugar substitute (Splenda recommended)
1 tablespoon wheat or oat bran
¼ teaspoon baking powder
½ cup fresh blueberries

> **YIELD:**
> 4 servings
>
> **NET CARBOHYDRATES:**
> 4 grams per serving
>
> **PREP:**
> 10 minutes
>
> **COOK:**
> 5 minutes

1. Grease a griddle or large skillet with cooking spray or butter and heat over medium heat for at least 5 minutes. The griddle should be very hot so that the pancakes don't stick.

2. Mix all the ingredients except the blueberries in a blender or food processor for about 15 seconds. Stop and scrape down the sides with a spatula, then mix for another 15 seconds until well blended.

3. Pour approximately 12 little cakes onto the hot griddle (they should be about the size of the bottom of a soda can). Wait for the pancakes to bubble, then sprinkle each with a few blueberries. Cook for a little longer, then flip with a spatula and cook for a few more minutes, until both sides of the pancakes are lightly browned. Serve hot with melted butter or top with a dollop of ***Stella Style*** Whipped Cream (page 231).

HELPFUL HINT

You may substitute any berry in this recipe but cut larger berries, such as strawberries, into smaller pieces.

Crêpes

Crêpes are terrific for breakfast, lunch, or my favorite—dessert! However you use them, these quick, easy-to-make crêpes come in handy all times of the day and night. We always make more than we need, then freeze the rest so we have them on hand when the urge strikes!

YIELD:
8 to 10 crepes,
2 per serving

NET CARBOHYDRATES:
2 grams per serving

PREP:
10 minutes

COOK:
2 minutes

¼ **cup ricotta cheese**
2 large eggs
2 tablespoons sugar substitute (Splenda recommended)
1½ **teaspoons ground cinnamon**
½ **teaspoon sugar-free vanilla extract**
2 tablespoons butter

1. Put all the ingredients except the butter into a bowl and mix well with a whisk.

2. Melt about 1 teaspoon of the butter in a small nonstick skillet over medium heat.

3. Drop 1 heaping tablespoon of the crêpe batter in the hot pan and immediately tilt the pan back and forth to spread the batter as thinly as possible. (You may make the crêpes as large as you like, but the larger they are, the more difficult they are to flip.)

4. Cook for about a minute, until set, then carefully flip the crêpe and cook for just a few more seconds until lightly browned. Repeat this procedure until you've used all the batter.

HELPFUL HINTS

Try stuffing these crêpe with cannoli cream (page 230), Strawberries and Cream Parfait (page 224), or fresh fruit and *Stella Style* Whipped Cream (page 231)! You can store any leftovers between sheets of parchment or waxed paper and keep them fresh in the refrigerator for a few days or freeze them.

Zucchini Blinis

A "blini" is a small pancake. In the restaurant I used to serve potato blinis with beluga caviar, but since Rachel doesn't often bring caviar home from the supermarket, we tend to eat these for breakfast as you would hash browns or for dinner in place of potatoes. Naturally, since this is **Stella Style,** we replaced the potato with zucchini in order to reinvent this classic!

2 large eggs
½ teaspoon salt
½ teaspoon baking powder
¼ teaspoon freshly ground black pepper
¼ teaspoon garlic powder
¼ cup soy flour
1 cup grated zucchini (use the largest holes on your
    cheese grater)
¼ cup grated Parmesan cheese
1 tablespoon minced red onion
2 tablespoons vegetable oil

YIELD:
4 servings

NET CARBOHYDRATES:
4 grams per serving

PREP:
15 minutes

COOK:
5 minutes

1. Put the eggs, salt, baking powder, pepper, and garlic powder into a bowl and mix well with a whisk.

2. Add the soy flour, zucchini, Parmesan cheese, and onion and whisk well.

3. Put a scant teaspoon of the oil in a small nonstick skillet over medium heat. Drop heaping tablespoon of the batter in the pan and cook for about 2 minutes on each side, until golden brown. When the blini is fully cooked, put it on a serving plate on the back of the stove to keep warm and repeat the process until you've made all 8 blinis. Serve hot.

HELPFUL HINT

These blinis are really great sprinkled with salt and dipped in Quick and Easy Ketchup (page 82)!

George's Gorgeous Macadamia Banana Muffins

Bananas are very high in carbs, so they're not a big part of eating **Stella Style,** but Rachel found a way to bring the great taste of bananas into these delicious muffins.

YIELD:
6 servings

NET CARBOHYDRATES:
8 grams per serving

PREP:
15 minutes

COOK:
25 minutes

Vegetable oil cooking spray
2 tablespoons wheat or oat bran
1 cup plus 1 tablespoon soy flour
$\frac{1}{2}$ cup sugar substitute (Splenda recommended)
1 teaspoon baking powder
2 large eggs
$\frac{1}{2}$ cup heavy cream
$\frac{1}{3}$ cup club soda
$1\frac{1}{2}$ teaspoons sugar-free banana extract
$\frac{1}{2}$ cup coarsely chopped macadamia nuts

Special equipment: 6-cup giant muffin tin

1. Place a rack in the center of the oven and preheat to 375° F.

2. Spray the muffin tin with cooking spray. Mix the bran with 1 tablespoon soy flour and evenly sprinkle the pan with the mixture, being especially careful to coat the sides of the cups (this will keep the muffins from sticking).

3. Whisk all the remaining ingredients except the nuts in a bowl until well blended, then fold in the nuts. Fill the 6 muffin cups evenly with the batter until they're about two-thirds full. Bake for 20 to 25 minutes, until the tops turn golden brown and a toothpick stuck in the center of a muffin comes out clean. Remove from the oven and allow to cool for 5 minutes. Serve the muffins warm with butter or cold with cream cheese. You can refrigerate or freeze any leftovers.

HELPFUL HINTS

Want to know an easy way to fill the large muffin cups? Use a regular ice cream scoop! They'll come out just the right size. And, of course, since it's **Stella Style,** you can use walnuts instead of macadamia nuts, if that's what you like!

Zucchini Muffins

These versatile little muffins can be toasted and smeared with butter or cream cheese for breakfast, served in place of bread for dinner, or even turned into strawberry shortcakes for dessert (page 225)!

Vegetable oil cooking spray
¼ cup wheat or oat bran
1½ cups plus 2 tablespoons soy flour
½ cup finely diced zucchini, with skin
3 large eggs
¾ cup heavy cream
½ cup club soda
⅓ cup sugar substitute (Splenda recommended)
1½ teaspoons baking powder

Special Equipment: 12-cup muffin tin

YIELD:
12 servings

NET CARBOHYDRATES:
6 grams per serving

PREP:
15 minutes

COOK:
25 minutes

1. Preheat the oven to 375° F.

2. Grease a 12-cup muffin tin with the cooking spray. In a small bowl, mix together the bran and 2 tablespoons soy flour. Evenly sprinkle the pan with the mixture, being careful to coat the sides.

3. In a larger bowl, whisk the remaining ingredients until completely blended. Fill muffin cups about two-thirds full with the batter.

4. Bake for 20 to 25 minutes, until the tops start to brown. (Be careful not to overcook or they will be very dry.) The muffins are done when lightly browned or when a toothpick inserted in the center of a muffin comes out clean.

5. Remove the muffins from the oven and let them cool for 5 minutes before removing from the tin. Serve warm with a pat of butter or at room temperature with cream cheese. Refrigerate any leftovers in a sealed container.

HELPFUL HINT

You can wrap and freeze these muffins individually for a microwave-ready anytime treat, or to grab and go in the morning!

Chocolate Chip Muffins

Rachel has become the Muffin Master of our household, and these are my absolute favorite of all her creations. I love them while they're hot from the oven and the chocolate chips are still melting. As an added bonus, the soy flour in the recipe is full of fiber—something we all need no matter how we eat! Serve them warm with butter or cold with a dab of cream cheese but, of course, they're great alone too!

YIELD:
6 servings

NET CARBOHYDRATES:
8 grams per serving

PREP:
15 minutes

COOK:
25 minutes

Vegetable oil cooking spray
2 tablespoons wheat or oat bran
1 cup plus 1 tablespoon soy flour
½ cup sugar substitute (Splenda recommended)
1 teaspoon baking powder
2 large eggs
½ cup heavy cream
⅓ cup club soda
½ cup *Stella Style* Chocolate Chips (page 209)

Special equipment: 6-cup muffin tin

1. Place the rack in the center of the oven and preheat to 375° F.

2. Spray the muffin tin with cooking spray. Mix the bran and 1 tablespoon soy flour and sprinkle the mixture evenly in each of the muffin cups, being careful to coat the sides. This will help prevent sticking.

3. Put all the remaining ingredients except the chocolate into a bowl and whisk until well blended, then gently fold in the chocolate chips. Fill the 6 muffin cups evenly about two-thirds full.

4. Bake for 20 to 25 minutes, until the muffin tops turn golden brown and a toothpick stuck in the center comes out clean.

5. Remove from the oven and let cool for 5 minutes before removing the muffins from the tin. Store any leftovers in a sealed container in the refrigerator.

HELPFUL HINT

Want to serve these for dessert? Just cut the top off each muffin, flip it over, and add chopped walnuts and a dollop of *Stella Style* Whipped Cream (page 231) to each half.

Ham and Cheddar Morning Muffins

Rachel makes these breakfast muffins, wraps them individually, and then freezes them. Whenever I don't feel like cooking in the morning, I grab one and pop it in the microwave while I make my morning coffee! It's easy to skip breakfast, and lunch, and dinner. Any person with a weight problem will tell you so. (Starving myself, believe it or not, was a big factor in my weight gain. What's really weird is that learning to eat again helped me shed those same pounds.) You gotta eat to lose weight! Breakfast especially! Preparing treats like these in advance—so they're ready when you are—is a great way to keep your furnace stoked and the calories burning!

YIELD:
12 servings

NET CARBOHYDRATES:
6 grams per serving

PREP:
15 minutes

COOK:
25 minutes

Vegetable oil cooking spray or butter
¼ cup wheat or oat bran (or additional soy flour)
1½ cups plus 2 tablespoons soy flour
¾ cup finely diced baked ham
½ cup shredded sharp Cheddar cheese
3 large eggs
¾ cup heavy cream
½ cup club soda
⅓ cup sugar substitute (Splenda recommended)
1½ teaspoons baking powder

Special Equipment: 12-cup muffin tin

1. Preheat the oven to 375° F.

2. Grease a 12-cup muffin tin with cooking spray or butter and set aside.

3. In a small bowl, mix together the bran and 2 tablespoons soy flour. Sprinkle the mixture evenly over each cup of the muffin pan. This will help keep the muffins from sticking.

4. In a larger bowl, whisk together the remaining ingredients until completely blended.

5. Fill each muffin cup about two-thirds with the batter (I use an ice cream scoop), leaving room for the muffins to rise.

6. Bake for 20 to 25 minutes, until the tops of the muffins start to brown. (Be careful not to overcook or they'll be very dry.) The muffins are done when lightly browned or when a wooden toothpick inserted into the center of a muffin comes out clean.

7. Remove the muffins from the oven and let them cool for 5 minutes before removing them from the tin. Serve warm with a pat of butter or at room temperature with cream cheese. Refrigerate any leftovers in a sealed container.

Rachel's Raspberry Muffins

I remember my mom making fresh muffins, cutting one in half right out of the oven, putting a pat of butter on it to melt, and handing it to me as I drooled on the counter! If you ask Rachel, she'll tell you that as she's baking these muffins, I do the same thing today, waiting for the oven timer to ring (or for Rachel to turn her back)!

YIELD:
6 servings

NET CARBOHYDRATES:
8 grams per serving

PREP:
15 minutes

COOK:
25 minutes

Vegetable oil cooking spray
2 tablespoons wheat or oat bran
1 cup plus 1 tablespoon soy flour
$\frac{1}{2}$ cup sugar substitute (Splenda recommended)
1 teaspoon baking powder
2 large eggs
$\frac{1}{2}$ cup heavy cream
$\frac{1}{3}$ cup club soda
$\frac{1}{2}$ cup fresh raspberries*

Special Equipment: 6-cup giant muffin tin

1. Place the baking rack in the center of the oven and preheat to 375° F.

2. Grease the muffin tin with cooking spray. Mix the bran together with 1 tablespoon soy flour and evenly sprinkle the pan with the mixture, being careful to coat the sides. This will prevent sticking.

3. In a bowl, whisk all the remaining ingredients except the raspberries until well blended. Fold in the raspberries (be gentle so they won't get crushed). Fill the muffin cups about two-thirds full with the batter, using an ice cream scoop.

4. Bake for 20 to 25 minutes, until the muffin tops turn golden brown and a toothpick stuck in the center comes out clean.

5. Remove the muffins from the oven and let them cool for 5 minutes before removing from the tin. Serve warm with a pat of butter or at room temperature with cream cheese. Refrigerate any leftovers in a sealed container.

*COOK'S TIP: If the raspberries aren't naturally sweet enough, sprinkle with an additional tablespoon of sugar substitute before folding them into the batter.

HELPFUL HINT

Try blueberries or blackberries instead of raspberries for a delicious change.

Spice Muffins with Cream Cheese Frosting

Rachel and I always loved frosted carrot cake, but that's off-limits when you're eating low carb. We created these muffins to fill that void, and the one in your stomach!

YIELD:
6 servings

NET CARBOHYDRATES:
8 grams per serving

PREP:
15 minutes

COOK:
25 minutes

Vegetable oil cooking spray
2 tablespoons wheat or oat bran
1 cup plus 1 tablespoon soy flour
$\frac{1}{2}$ cup sugar substitute (Splenda recommended)
$1\frac{1}{2}$ teaspoons sugar-free vanilla extract
$1\frac{1}{2}$ teaspoons ground allspice
1 teaspoon baking powder
2 large eggs
$\frac{1}{2}$ cup heavy cream
$\frac{1}{3}$ cup club soda
$\frac{1}{2}$ cup chopped pecans
6 ounces Cream Cheese Frosting (page 233)

Special equipment: 6-cup giant muffin tin

1. Place the rack in the center of the oven and preheat to 375° F.

2. Spray the muffin tin with cooking spray. Mix together the bran and 1 tablespoon soy flour. Evenly sprinkle the pan with the mixture, being careful to coat the sides of the cups. This will help prevent sticking.

3. In a bowl, whisk all the remaining ingredients until well blended. Fill the muffin cups about two-thirds full with the batter, using an ice cream scoop.

4. Bake for 20 to 25 minutes, until the tops of the muffins turn golden brown and a toothpick stuck in the center comes out clean.

5. Remove from the oven and let cool completely before frosting.

6. Frost the tops of the muffins generously with cream cheese frosting, refrigerate, and serve cold. Leftovers will stay fresh in the refrigerator for 3 days.

HELPFUL HINTS

If you want to bring these muffins to a friend's house as a hostess gift, refrigerate the frosted muffins for 1 hour before lightly covering with plastic wrap so that the wrap doesn't stick to the frosted tops. You can also freeze these muffins for an anytime snack, but frost them after thawing, not before freezing.

Frittata Italiana

You say Potato, I say Frittata! I first whipped this up one Mother's Day while making breakfast for Rachel. As usual, I found out that the kids loved it too! This Italian Frittata is chock full of the flavors I grew up with in my grandmother's kitchen. It is a welcome change for breakfast, lunch—or, when you're eating *Stella Style*—anytime!

YIELD:
8 servings

NET CARBOHYDRATES:
3 grams per serving

PREP:
15 minutes

COOK:
15 minutes

6 ounces fresh Italian sausage, crumbled out of the casing
¼ cup diced red onion
2 Roma tomatoes, seeded and diced
½ teaspoon minced fresh garlic
2 tablespoons butter
½ cup shredded sharp Cheddar cheese
¾ cup grated Parmesan cheese
2 tablespoons diced roasted red bell pepper
2 tablespoons sliced black olives
2 tablespoons chopped fresh basil

EGG MIXTURE:
10 large eggs
¼ cup heavy cream
¼ cup water
1 teaspoon dried oregano
½ teaspoon salt
¼ teaspoon grated nutmeg (freshly ground nutmeg
    is always best!)

1. Preheat the oven to 325° F.

2. In a sauté pan over medium-high heat, brown the crumbled Italian sausage with the onion, tomatoes, and garlic. Drain off the excess fat using a spoon or turkey baster.

3. Place all the ingredients for the egg mixture in a bowl and whisk well.

4. Melt the butter in a large ovenproof skillet over medium-high heat.

5. Pour the egg mixture into the pan. Using a rubber spatula, slowly push the cooked egg from one side of the pan to the other to allow all of the raw egg to reach the bottom of the pan (this creates height and keeps the bottom from burning).

6. When the frittata is cooked on the bottom but the top is still runny, spoon the cooked sausage mixture, the cheeses, and red pepper over the top.

7. Cover the pan with aluminum foil and bake for 12 to 15 minutes. (Remove the foil for the last few minutes of cooking for a nicely browned top.) The frittata is done when firm and a toothpick stuck in the center comes out clean.

8. Cut into 8 servings and serve hot, garnished with the black olives and basil.

On-Hand Omelet

I was going to call this recipe Leftover Omelet, but I didn't want anyone to think they should keep omelets in their fridge for days! What I mean to say is that whatever you have on hand from dinner the night before can easily be turned into a great morning starter the day after. So scour your refrigerator and serve it up—*Stella Style!*

YIELD:
2 servings

NET CARBOHYDRATES:
3 grams per serving
(with ingredients listed
below)

PREP:
15 minutes

COOK:
10 minutes

3 ounces thinly sliced cooked steak (you can also use chicken or whatever other protein you had for dinner the night before)

2 ounces cooked spinach (or any other low-carb veggie you find in the fridge)

5 large eggs

2 tablespoons half-and-half (you can also use water, but cream makes eggs fluffier)

1/8 teaspoon baking powder

1/8 teaspoon salt

1/8 teaspoon freshly ground black pepper

1 tablespoon unsalted butter

3 ounces shredded Cheddar cheese (or whatever other cheese is on hand)

1. Preheat the broiler to high.

2. Warm up the steak and spinach in a sauté pan or in the microwave.

3. Place the eggs, half-and-half, baking powder, salt, and pepper in a blender or food processor and process on high speed for about 10 seconds to incorporate air into the mix (the half-and-half and baking powder will help the omelet rise). You can also use a hand-held blender to mix the ingredients in a deep bowl.

4. Melt the butter in a large, ovenproof, nonstick skillet over medium-high heat. Pour in the egg mixture. Using a rubber spatula, slowly push the cooked egg from one side of the pan to the other to allow the raw egg to reach the bottom of the pan and cook (this creates height and keeps the bottom from burning).

5. When the omelet is cooked on the bottom but the top is still runny, you can either flip the omelet in the pan to finish or, to make the omelet rise even more, place the pan just below the broiler with the oven door open and the handle sticking out for about 30 seconds, until the omelet rises and lightly browns.

6. Remove the omelet from the heat, add the warmed filling and the cheese, and fold in half. To serve, cut into pieces. If you wish, save a little filling and cheese to put on top after folding.

HELPFUL HINT

Making an omelet is one time you really should use a nonstick pan because the surface really does allow the eggs to cook without sticking, which is essential for an intact omelet. If you want, you can cut back on the butter or use vegetable oil cooking spray instead.

Kitchen Sink Quiche

Real men really do eat quiche! I love it hot, and I love it cold! Like all **Stella Style** entrées, it's good for a grab-and-go breakfast, great for lunch, and comes in handy as a late-night snack too! Have any leftovers hiding behind the half-and-half? Simply throw them into the Kitchen Sink Quiche, and watch your weight go down the drain!

YIELD:
12 servings

NET CARBOHYDRATES:
2 grams per serving

PREP:
15 minutes

COOK:
40 minutes

Vegetable oil cooking spray
8 large eggs
1 cup heavy cream
¼ teaspoon kosher salt
⅛ teaspoon freshly ground black pepper
⅛ teaspoon ground white pepper
Pinch of ground nutmeg
1 cup shredded sharp Cheddar cheese (or 1 cup similar cheese)
1 cup shredded Swiss cheese (or 1 cup similar cheeses)
1 cup coarsely crumbled cooked bacon (you may also use meat or poultry leftovers, such as ham, turkey, chicken, or steak, or just leave them out if you're eating vegetarian)
1 cup leftover low-carb veggies (such as broccoli, cauliflower, spinach, squash, zucchini, asparagus, roasted peppers, or mushrooms), cut into small pieces
2 tablespoons chopped green onion (scallion) tops

Special equipment: 8-inch glass pie pan

1. Preheat the oven to 350° F. Spray the pie pan with cooking spray.

2. Mix the eggs, cream, salt, both peppers, and the nutmeg in a bowl, then pour the mixture into the pie pan.

3. Sprinkle the cheese, bacon (if using), and vegetables over the top, then push them down into the egg mixture with your hands or the back of a spoon, spreading the fillings evenly.

4. Bake for about 40 minutes, until the top of the quiche turns golden brown and a toothpick stuck in the center comes out clean. Let rest for 15 minutes to allow the quiche to set before slicing it. Garnish with the scallion and serve.

HELPFUL HINT

Quiche holds up well in the fridge for a couple of days, so make more than one to have handy for lunches and snacks!

Rachel's Raspberry Muffins (p. 38);
On-Hand Omelet with chicken, chard,
and white Cheddar cheese (p. 44)

Southern Fried Chicken (p. 132); Waldorf Cole Slaw (p. 195); Old-Fashioned Egg Mock Potato Salad (p. 187)

Low-Carb Pizza (p. 58)

Anaheim Shrimp Scampi (p. 144); Zucchini, Yellow Squash, and Tomato Fromage (p. 186)

Roasted Rosemary Pork Loin (p. 123); Grilled Summer Vegetables (p. 184); Radicchio Salad with Quick Raspberry Vinaigrette (p. 170)

Teriyaki Ginger Garlic Chicken Satay (p. 76); Nutty Muddy Trail Mix (p. 52); White Wine Spritzers (p. 200)

*Stella Style New York
Ricotta Cheesecake (p. 216)*

Neapolitan Parfaits (p. 228); Praline Pumpkin Pie with fresh whipped cream (p. 222)

Snacks

For years, we've been told to cut back on snacks in order to lose weight. According to the experts, snacking is why we all weigh so much! (I must have heard that line at least ten times a day before I started low-carbing, and you know what? I believed it!)

Imagine my surprise when I found out that the "experts" had it all wrong. You've got to eat to lose weight, and that means you've got to snack between meals in order to control your cravings. It wasn't snacking that was bad for me; it was the food I was snacking on!

Any nutritionist will tell you that you should try to keep something in your stomach all day long, instead of first starving and then stuffing yourself. Healthy, satisfying snacks are an important ingredient in *Stella Style,* and you have to learn how to make them—and how to take them on the road—in order to steer clear of trouble between meals.

For some of us, the greatest temptations of the day come during the time we spend at work. Food, after all, is one of the first things we reach for when we're stressed out. (Think about how cigarettes, and even coffee, serve almost the same purpose, and how when you quit smoking, you tend to eat more than ever!) So what do we eat when we're at work, far from the safety of our own kitchens? Junk, that's what!

We eat doughnuts in the morning, drink sugary soda all day long, eat fast food for lunch, and grab candy bars in the afternoon. Once again, in order to change the way we eat, we have to change the food we keep within reach. So why not try taking some of **Renee's Roasted Cinnamon Candied Nuts,** or my **Nutty Muddy Trail Mix**

Renee's Roasted
Cinnamon
Candied Nuts

Nutty Muddy Trail Mix

Steph's Sweet Deli Rolls

Crispy Pepperoni Chips

Don't Be Blue (Berries)

Refreshing Fruit Kebabs

Low-Carb Pizza

with you to work? Or, if there's a refrigerator at work that you can use, how about making some of my sister **Steph's Sweet Deli Rolls** and bringing them into work with you? (Watch out, though! If the boss gets to them first, you just might find yourself out of a job if you don't keep the supply of delicious, low-carb snacks coming!)

At home the problem is exactly the same, but the solutions are far more numerous. You can keep some **Refreshing Fruit Kebabs** in the refrigerator or some **Don't Be Blue (Berries)** in the freezer for whenever the urge to snack strikes you. And don't forget to raid my **Morning Starters** section for muffins! The important thing, once again, is to eat when you're hungry, and to stop when you feel satisfied. That's snacking—*Stella Style!*

Renee's Roasted Cinnamon Candied Nuts

Rachel's sister Renee made these for us one Christmas, and they were so outrageously tasty I just had to have the recipe! (I did have my own recipe for roasted nuts, but this one was the best I'd ever tasted.) Hey, I'm good, but I know when I'm beat!

Vegetable oil cooking spray
1 large egg white
1½ teaspoons water
¾ cup sugar substitute (Splenda recommended)
½ teaspoon ground cinnamon
2 cups assorted whole natural almonds, walnuts halves, and pecan halves

YIELD: 12 servings, 1½ ounces per serving
NET CARBOHYDRATES: 2 grams per serving
PREP: 15 minutes
COOK: 25 minutes

1. Preheat the oven to 325° F.

2. Cut a brown paper bag to size and use it to line a cookie sheet. Spray the top surface of the paper heavily with cooking spray.

3. Whisk the egg white in a bowl until frothy. Add the water, sugar substitute, and cinnamon and whisk thoroughly.

4. Add the nuts to the egg white mixture and toss to coat well.

5. Spread the coated nuts in a single layer on the oil-coated paper and bake for 20 to 25 minutes. Remove and allow to cool before breaking apart.

6. Store the candied nuts in a sealed container (do not refrigerate). I was gonna tell you how long they'll last on your countertop before I thought, who am I kidding? They don't last at all—everyone eats them!

Nutty Muddy Trail Mix

Why "muddy"? Because these mixed nuts are covered in mud! (Not really, but when chefs put tons of spices into a dish—say, for example, rice—we call it "dirty" rice. By that logic, these are "muddy" nuts.) These great low-carb nuts are so covered in spices they could almost be called filthy! So fire up the oven, put on some old clothes, and get dirty!

YIELD:
24 servings,
1½ ounces each

NET CARBOHYDRATES:
2 grams per serving

PREP:
10 minutes

COOK:
20 minutes

1 cup whole natural almonds (you can find these in the produce department or baking section at the grocery store or at your local health food store)

1 cup pecan halves

1 cup walnut halves

½ cup unsalted shelled sunflower seeds

½ cup unsalted shelled pumpkin seeds

4 tablespoons butter, melted

½ teaspoon salt

½ teaspoon garlic powder

½ teaspoon chili powder

½ teaspoon ground cumin

2 pinches of cayenne pepper

1. Preheat the oven to 350° F.

2. In a large bowl, mix together the nuts, seeds, melted butter, and all the seasonings. Toss to coat well.

3. Spread the coated nuts in a single layer on a baking sheet and bake for 15 to 20 minutes. Shake the pan every few minutes while cooking to make sure the nuts cook evenly on all sides. Remove from the oven and let cool. Store any leftovers in an airtight container.

HELPFUL HINT

If you don't have all the different kinds of nuts, just use what you have! There are no set rules! Feel free to substitute peanuts, cashews, or macadamia nuts.

Steph's Sweet Deli Rolls

We low-carbers are always sharing ideas, especially for last-minute snack ideas. This one just happens to come from my sister Stephanie, who, after seeing our family lose so much weight, started eating *Stella Style* herself. She lost a bunch of weight and continues to share her discoveries with us. (Once she sees her name in print, I'll bet she's going to send me a bunch more recipes—so keep an eye out!)

8 ounces cream cheese, softened to room temperature
¼ cup sugar-free sweet pickle relish (we use Mt. Olive brand, available at most major grocery stores)
2 tablespoons diced red onion
4 slices deli ham
4 slices deli turkey breast
1 seedless cucumber, with peel, sliced into rounds (optional)

YIELD:
8 servings

NET CARBOHYDRATES:
5 grams per serving

PREP:
15 minutes

CHILL:
1 hour

1. Combine the cream cheese, pickle relish, and red onion in a bowl until completely blended.

2. Spread a thin layer of the cream cheese mixture over each piece of deli meat, then roll it up like a jellyroll.

3. Refrigerate for 1 hour to firm, then cut each roll crosswise into 3 slices.

4. If you like, place each piece atop a cucumber round (the perfect low-carb alternative to crackers) to serve!

HELPFUL HINT

Let your kids lend a hand. They just love to make these!

Crispy Pepperoni Chips

Rachel is standing right behind me as I write this recipe. She says that she wanted something crunchy one night—something like potato chips—and she started turning over the possibilities in her mind. What could be sliced, just like a potato, into thin chips? She opened the refrigerator door, and the first thing she saw was a stick of pepperoni. The rest is history! (At the bottom of the recipe, I've included a few ideas for the leftovers, but Rachel says I shouldn't have bothered, since there won't be any!)

YIELD:
4 servings

NET CARBOHYDRATES:
0 grams per serving

PREP:
5 minutes

COOK:
10 to 15 minutes

6 ounces pepperoni, thinly sliced

1. Preheat the oven to 425° F.

2. Lay the pepperoni slices in a single layer on a baking sheet and bake for 8 to 10 minutes.

3. Remove the pan from the oven and soak up the excess grease by pressing paper towels against the pepperoni chips. Return the pan to the oven and bake an additional 2 to 4 minutes, until the pepperoni slices are very crispy.

HELPFUL HINTS

Serve as a snack anytime or use in place of crackers for dipping or for topping with your favorite cheese! They'll stay fresh and crispy for a day or two if you store them in an airtight container.

Don't Be Blue (Berries)

I used to love going to the movies and buying the big box of my favorite candy—Raisinettes! One day Rachel froze some blueberries that were about to go bad. When I found them in the freezer, I decided to dip them in our sugar-free Chocolate Ganache. I couldn't believe my taste buds—they tasted exactly like Raisinettes! Freezing the blueberries gives them a raisiny texture, and when you dip them in *Stella Style* chocolate . . . well, let's just say you'll never be blue with these chocolate-covered berries!

½ **cup fresh blueberries, stems removed**
Chocolate Ganache (page 214)

1. Lay the blueberries in a flat dish lined with waxed paper and freeze for at least 30 minutes.

2. While the blueberries are freezing, make the Chocolate Ganache.

3. Dip the frozen blueberries a couple at a time into the warm chocolate, then remove them quickly with a fork and return them to the waxed paper. Spread them around so that they don't stick together in big bunches, then put them back into the freezer for just a couple more minutes. Serve frozen.

HELPFUL HINTS

Another way to make these is to put the frozen blueberries on a plate, pour the warm ganache over top, and separate the berries with a fork. Once all the berries are coated, freeze them for a few more minutes. Serve frozen and do your best to eat them before they melt (or ask someone for help)!

YIELD:
4 servings
NET CARBOHYDRATES:
5 grams per serving
PREP:
15 minutes
CHILL:
35 minutes

Refreshing Fruit Kebabs

I put everything I can on the grill, and I mean everything! These fruit kebabs are refreshingly different and proof that you can have plenty of fruit when you're eating *Stella Style!*

YIELD:
8 servings:

NET CARBOHYDRATES:
5 grams per serving

PREP:
10 minutes

COOK:
3 minutes

1 whole cantaloupe (¹/₂ for the kebabs, ¹/₂ for display)
1 whole honeydew melon (¹/₂ for the kebabs, ¹/₂ for display)
2 pints fresh strawberries, hulled
2 tablespoons shredded fresh coconut, optional

Special equipment: Eight 8-inch bamboo skewers
Outdoor grill, indoor grill top, or grill pan

1. Soak the bamboo skewers in water for 30 minutes to keep them from burning while on the grill.

2. Preheat the grill to medium-high or heat an indoor grill top or grill pan over high heat.

3. Cut both melons in half, scoop out the seeds, and reserve half of each kind of melon for display.

4. Trim the rinds off the other melon halves, then cut the melon into 2-inch chunks. (Try and cut each melon piece as close to the same size as possible, so they'll cook evenly.)

5. Leaving about 2 inches of bamboo at the bottom of the skewer, alternately thread pieces of cantaloupe, strawberry, and honeydew on each skewer, finishing each one with a strawberry about 1 inch from the blunt end.

6. Place the kebabs on the edges of the grill with the bare part of the skewers hanging off the edge away from the fire. Watch closely, since the skewers will cook very quickly. Turn the skewers to the next side before they begin to burn until all four sides are cooked. The kebabs will be done in just 2 to 3 minutes—any longer and they will fall apart.

7. Remove the kebabs and sprinkle with the shredded coconut. With a melon baller, cut melon balls from the remaining melon halves. Return the melon balls to the scooped-out melons halves, then stick the grilled kebabs around the sides for a festive presentation.

Low-Carb Pizza

We first made this pizza for a few hundred people on the Atkins cruise years ago. Hundreds of people crashed our pizza party, saying our pizzas looked better than the ones the ship was serving! Rachel scared them all away by telling them it was "diet food." Diet food? I don't think so. It's just one more great way to enjoy comfort food while living *Stella Style!*

YIELD:
16 servings

NET CARBOHYDRATES:
6 grams per serving

PREP:
35 minutes

COOK:
30 minutes

Vegetable oil cooking spray

CRUST:

1½ cups soy flour

3 large eggs

¾ cup heavy cream

⅓ cup club soda

1 teaspoon salt

MARINARA SAUCE:

1 tablespoon olive oil

2 tablespoons diced red onion

1 teaspoon finely chopped garlic

3 large Roma tomatoes, diced

One 8-ounce can sugar free tomato sauce

¼ teaspoon garlic powder

½ teaspoon dried basil

½ teaspoon dried oregano (you may substitute Italian seasoning for the dried herbs)

⅛ teaspoon salt

⅛ teaspoon freshly ground black pepper

TOPPINGS:

1½ pounds mozzarella cheese, shredded

12 ounces pepperoni, sliced

⅓ cup julienned red bell pepper

⅓ cup julienned green bell pepper

⅓ cup julienned red onion

2 portobello mushroom caps, sliced

2 tablespoons extra-virgin olive oil
2 pinches of dried oregano

Special equipment: Two 12-inch pizza pans

1. Place the rack in the center of the oven and preheat to 375° F. Generously spray the pizza pans with cooking spray.

2. Make the crusts: In a medium bowl, stir together all of the crust ingredients to make a smooth, thick, batter.

3. Using a rubber spatula, spread half the batter as thinly and evenly as possible over the first pan. Repeat with the second pan.

4. Bake the pizza crusts for 12 to 15 minutes, until light golden brown and firm to the touch. Remove the crusts from the oven and increase the oven temperature to 400° F.

5. While the crusts are baking, make the sauce: Heat the olive oil in a small saucepan over medium heat. Add the onion and garlic and cook just until softened and translucent, about 2 minutes. Add the tomatoes along with the remaining sauce ingredients and simmer for about 2 minutes.

6. Top the pizzas: Spread half the tomato sauce and half the mozzarella cheese over each crust. Top one pizza with the pepperoni and the other with the bell pepper strips, onion, and mushrooms if you want to offer guests a vegetarian option. Otherwise, scatter all toppings evenly over both pizzas. Lightly drizzle 1 tablespoon olive oil over each pizza and sprinkle each with a pinch of dried oregano.

7. Return the pizzas to the oven and bake for 10 to 12 minutes, until the cheese melts and starts to brown. Remove and cut each pizza into 8 slices before serving.

HELPFUL HINT

Make sure to bake the pizza crusts until they're really golden brown the first time you put them in the oven. That will ensure a crispier crust after they are baked with the toppings!

Appetizers

Stella Style means eating anything, anytime—as long as it's low in carbs and high in flavor. Don't forget that even though we've put the following recipes in the **Appetizers** section, you can have them for breakfast, lunch, or dinner. **Jimi's Fried Mozzarella Sticks** are a perfect example, and so are our **Crab-Stuffed Mushrooms** and "**If You Had Wings**" **Chicken Wings**! Plus, you can always sneak a recipe like our **Low-Carb Pizza**, made with Rachel's soy-flour pizza crust, from the **Snacks** category, cut it into smaller pieces, and serve those up as a terrific appetizer too!

So grab the deli meats and cheeses and make yourself a **Last-Minute Antipasto Platter**! Or some **BLT Roll-Ups**. Just watch that you don't put too many of these out at a dinner party, because these **Appetizers** are so good your guests might not have room for the main course!

Fresh Fruit and Cheese
Martinis

Guacamole

BLT Roll-Ups

Smoked Salmon
Pinwheels

Teriyaki Sesame
Tuna Skewers

Crab-Stuffed
Mushrooms

Last-Minute Antipasto
Platter

Wild Mushroom Ragout

"If You Had Wings"
Chicken Wings

Jimi's Fried Mozzarella
Sticks

Teriyaki Ginger Garlic
Chicken Satay

Fresh Fruit and Cheese Martinis

This combination of fresh berries, fruits, nuts, and ricotta cheese was the lucky result of a late-night trial-and-error session. (Rachel must have thought I was nuts, and she was right. I am nuts—for this recipe!) Sometimes you just have to try something new. Why don't you try this martini before dinner as an "aperitif," or afterwards as a dessert! Cheers!

YIELD:
6 servings

NET CARBOHYDRATES:
5 grams per serving

PREP:
15 minutes

½ cup ricotta cheese
2 tablespoons sugar substitute (Splenda recommended)
½ cup small cantaloupe balls
½ cup small honeydew melon balls
⅓ cup blueberries
½ cup strawberries, sliced
2 tablespoons dry Champagne, optional
1 teaspoon freshly grated lemon zest (don't use dried)
1 tablespoon chopped pecans
Strawberries and blueberries, for garnish

1. In a bowl, whisk together the ricotta and 1 tablespoon of the sugar substitute.

2. In a separate bowl, combine the fruit and remaining 1 tablespoon sugar substitute with the Champagne (if using).

3. Place 2 heaping tablespoons of the fruit mixture into each of 6 martini glasses and top each one with 1 heaping tablespoon of the ricotta mixture.

4. Sprinkle the martinis with lemon zest and pecans.

5. To garnish, use a frilled toothpick or sword pick to skewer a strawberry and a couple blueberries and stick it into the top of each martini. Remember, if you're driving there's a two-drink limit!

Guacamole

Rachel almost always has an avocado ripening on the kitchen windowsill. They're great just cut up as a snack, and they're delicious in salads, but they're superb as guacamole! We love to use guacamole as a dip with pork rinds or serve it alongside our *Stella Style* quesadillas (page 154). Whatever way you choose, you can't go wrong, since avocados are loaded with good fats and vitamins that contribute to a healthy lifestyle!

1 ripe avocado (we prefer Hass, but any variety will do)
⅓ cup sour cream
1 tablespoon chopped red onion
1 small clove garlic, minced
1 tablespoon finely chopped fresh cilantro leaves
1 teaspoon fresh lime juice
Pinch of cayenne pepper
Salt and freshly ground black pepper to taste

YIELD:
4 servings

NET CARBOHYDRATES:
2 grams per serving

PREP:
10 minutes

1. Cut the avocado in half around the pit, twist it apart, and remove the pit.

2. Use a spoon to scoop the avocado pulp out of the skin into a medium bowl and mash the pulp.

3. Add the remaining ingredients and mix together until blended. Cover the surface of the guacamole with plastic wrap (this keeps your dip from darkening due to exposure to air) and refrigerate until ready to serve.

BLT Roll-Ups

These roll-ups are perfect way to get your kids interested in eating **Stella Style**. Our son Christian uses them as toppings for his salads, packs them for lunch, or eats them as a quick snack—both at home and on the road!

YIELD:
4 servings

NET CARBOHYDRATES:
1 gram per serving

PREP:
8 minutes

4 teaspoons mayonnaise
4 large leaves iceberg lettuce
4 ounces (8 slices) sugar-free turkey breast
4 ounces (8 slices) cooked bacon slices
4 ounces (8 slices) sliced Swiss cheese
1 ripe tomato, cut into 8 slices

Special equipment: Toothpicks

1. Spread 1 teaspoon mayonnaise on the inside of each leaf of iceberg lettuce. Top each leaf with 2 slices turkey, 2 slices bacon, 2 slices cheese, and 2 slices tomato.

2. Roll up like a jellyroll and secure with toothpicks.

3. Slice the rolls into ½-inch pinwheels.

HELPFUL HINT

You can pop the turkey, bacon, and cheese in the microwave, then roll everything up for a hot wrap with melted cheese. You'll love the contrast between the crisp, cold lettuce and tomato and the hot goodies inside!

Smoked Salmon Pinwheels

In the old days, I would go out to the buffets and eat my weight in smoked salmon! I especially liked it served traditionally, with capers, cream cheese, and onions. The only problem was that the capers and onions always fell off the fork when I tried to eat it all together. This recipe combines all my favorite ingredients in an easy-to-make and easy-to-serve party appetizer!

8 ounces cream cheese, softened
1 tablespoon fresh lemon juice
2 tablespoons diced red onion
1 tablespoon chopped fresh basil
8 ounces sliced smoked salmon (we recommend Nova,
    but you may use the saltier lox)
2 tablespoons small capers, drained
1 seedless cucumber, with peel, sliced into rounds the size
    of crackers

YIELD:
4 servings

NET CARBOHYDRATES:
1 gram per serving

PREP:
15 minutes

CHILL:
1 hour

1. Combine the cream cheese, lemon juice, red onion, and basil in a bowl until completely blended.

2. On a piece of waxed paper, arrange the smoked salmon slices in a rectangle about 3 inches wide and 12 inches long, slightly overlapping each piece. (If the salmon slices are cut irregularly, simply piece them together like a puzzle.)

3. Spread a thin layer of the cream cheese mixture on the salmon, sprinkle with the capers, and roll up like a jellyroll.

4. Refrigerate for 1 hour to firm, then cut into ½-inch slices.

5. Place each pinwheel atop a cucumber round to serve.

HELPFUL HINT

Use cucumber rounds in place of crackers for all your appetizers. Five cucumber rounds have less than 1 carb!

Teriyaki Sesame Tuna Skewers

I love tuna and anything teriyaki! So it was natural for me to put the two together. These skewers make great party appetizers or can be part of a more elaborate Chinese meal. Just serve them on top of Christian's Szechuan Vegetable Stir-Fry (page 152) with a side Ginger Salad (page 166), and you're eating Pacific Rim—*Stella Style!* With this recipe, you'll have a few skewers left over to snack on before you serve. Enjoy!

YIELD:
4 servings

NET CARBOHYDRATES:
4 grams per serving

PREP:
20 minutes

MARINATE:
30 minutes

COOK:
4 minutes

MARINADE:

15 ounces teriyaki sauce (average 2 grams sugar per serving)
6 tablespoons sesame oil
1 tablespoon minced fresh ginger
1 teaspoon minced fresh garlic
2 to 3 tablespoons fresh lemon juice (juice from 1 lemon)
1 tablespoon sugar substitute (Splenda recommended)

2 pounds fresh tuna steak, cut into 1-inch cubes
1 tablespoon sesame seeds, toasted*

Special equipment: thirty 8-inch bamboo skewers
Grill or grill pan

1. Soak the bamboo skewers in water for 30 minutes. (This will keep them from burning later.)

2. Mix all the marinade ingredients together in a nonreactive bowl. Place the tuna cubes in the marinade, cover, shake gently to mix, and refrigerate for at least 30 minutes.

3. Preheat a grill (or grill pan) to high.

4. Remove the tuna from the marinade and the skewers from the water, then thread the tuna onto the skewers, leaving 1 inch bare at the blunt end.

5. Place the skewers around the edges of the grill with the bare part of the skewers hanging off the edge away from the fire. Watch the skewers carefully as they cook very quickly. Turn them after a minute or two to cook the other side; the entire skewer will cook through in just 3 to 4 minutes.

6. Sprinkle the skewers with the toasted sesame seeds before serving.

*COOK'S TIP: To toast sesame seeds, heat a small skillet until hot. Add the raw seeds and stir gently with a wooden spoon until they brown and begin to pop. Remove from the heat and let cool.

HELPFUL HINT

For a more dramatic presentation, cut a cantaloupe in half, hollow it out with a melon baller, and place it on a platter as if were a bowl. Fill it up with the melon balls, then stick the skewers around the rim of the cantaloupe bowl.

Crab-Stuffed Mushrooms

I first made these mushrooms while working as a caterer many years ago. The recipe is still the same. I haven't had to change a single ingredient, and it's all low-carb! These will be the hit of the party, so make as many as you can, and then be sure to grab some yourself before they're all gone!

YIELD:
4 servings

NET CARBOHYDRATES:
2 grams per serving

PREP:
15 minutes

COOK:
20 minutes

Vegetable oil cooking spray
8 ounces cream cheese, softened to room temperature
8 ounces lump crabmeat*
$\frac{1}{3}$ cup grated Parmesan cheese
1 tablespoon chopped fresh parsley
1 teaspoon poultry seasoning
$\frac{1}{4}$ teaspoon freshly ground black pepper
$\frac{1}{8}$ teaspoon minced fresh garlic (you may also use garlic powder)
$\frac{1}{8}$ teaspoon salt
16 medium-sized white button mushrooms (about 1 pound)
2 tablespoons thinly sliced green onion (scallion) tops, for garnish

1. Preheat the oven to 350° F. Spray a baking sheet with cooking spray.

2. Combine all the ingredients except the mushrooms and green onions in a bowl.

3. Wipe the mushrooms clean with a damp cloth** and carefully twist the stems off. (You can save the stems for omelets!)

4. Fill each mushroom cap with a heaping spoonful of the crabmeat stuffing and line them filling side up on the greased baking sheet.

5. Spray cooking spray over all the stuffed mushrooms to keep them from drying out and bake for about 20 minutes, until the mushrooms are tender. Serve hot on a plate sprinkled with the sliced green onions.

*COOK'S TIP: You can use any real crabmeat in this recipe, but do NOT use artificial crab or surimi, because they almost always have added sugars. If you can't find lump crabmeat, buy a couple of King crab legs, crack them open, and remove the meat. It's cheaper in the long run—and really, really good!

**COOK'S TIP: Always wipe mushrooms clean (or use a mushroom cleaning brush) instead of rinsing them in water; mushrooms will absorb any water you wash them in and become spongy.

HELPFUL HINTS

You can make these hours ahead; just keep them tightly covered with plastic wrap in the refrigerator before baking. When you're ready for the final step, take them out of the fridge and let them warm to room temperature for a few minutes before you pop them in the preheated oven. There are never any leftovers!

Last-Minute Antipasto Platter

Looking for a quick-and-easy, last-minute, pick-it-up-at-the-store-on-your-way-there culinary feast for the eyes! Follow these guidelines, and you'll get an endless stream of compliments for doing nothing more than displaying these delicious low-carb ingredients when you show up at a party. When you arrive with this wonderful array of Italian meats, cheeses, and vegetables, there's only one thing left to do—*mangia!*

YIELD:
12 or more servings

NET CARBOHYDRATES:
3 grams per serving

PREP:
15 minutes

6 ounces "baby" or fresh mozzarella, cut into bite-sized pieces

4 ounces prosciutto, thinly sliced

4 ounces mortadella, thinly sliced

4 ounces capocollo, thinly sliced

5 to 6 ounces Asiago or aged provolone cheese

1 small stick sopressata (dried Italian sausage)

1 small stick pepperoni

1 small jar (6 ounces) marinated artichoke hearts

4 ounces oil-cured black olives (or substitute your favorite oil-cured olive)

1 small jar (6 ounces) pepperoncini peppers

6 ounces roasted red peppers (or 2 whole peppers), cut into bite-sized pieces

1 bunch fresh basil

1 teaspoon minced fresh garlic

2 tablespoons olive oil

1 seedless cucumber, with peel, thinly sliced

1. Use a separate cutting board for prepping and place a nice serving board for the display in front of you. Unwrap all the meats and cheeses and lay them out next to your display board.

2. Place the mozzarella in a small dish and set it on one corner of the serving board.

3. Roll up each slice of prosciutto like a jellyroll. Fold each slice of mortadella in half two or three times like an envelope. Wrap each slice of capocollo into a horn shape. Place the meats along the edges of the display board, alternating one after the other.

4. Cut the cheese, sopressata, and pepperoni into thin slices and place them on the display board inside the border of the folded meats. Scatter the board with the artichoke hearts, olives, pepperoncini, and roasted red peppers.

5. Take 5 or 6 basil leaves, stack them, roll the stack lengthwise into a tube like a cigar, and slice the tube into fine ribbons to make a chiffonade. Mix the chiffonade with the garlic and olive oil. Drizzle the mixture over the entire board.

6. Garnish with whole basil leaves and serve with a side plate of cucumber slices (these are terrific alternative to crackers or bread).

HELPFUL HINT

We always make a big display and use the leftovers for late-night snacking or breakfast the next day!

Wild Mushroom Ragout

Ragout is a fancy name for this old favorite of mine from the '80s—Scampi-Style Sautéed Mushrooms. It doesn't get any easier than this, or any better! This is a spectacular gourmet appetizer that you can make in just a few minutes!

YIELD:
4 servings

NET CARBOHYDRATES:
1 gram per serving

PREP:
15 minutes

COOK:
5 minutes

8 ounces small button mushrooms
8 ounces assorted mushrooms*
5 tablespoons Scampi Butter (page 88)
2 tablespoons chopped fresh parsley
1 lemon, cut into wedges

1. Wipe the mushrooms clean with a damp cloth. Trim any dirty or dried stems and discard.

2. Place 3 tablespoons of the scampi butter in a large sauté pan over medium heat.

3. Add the mushrooms and sauté for 4 or 5 minutes, until the mushrooms are fully cooked.

4. Remove from the heat and quickly stir in the remaining scampi butter. Divide among 4 small plates or bowls with rims. Sprinkle the parsley on top of the mushrooms or around the rims of the bowls and garnish with fresh lemon wedges.

*COOK'S TIP: I buy whatever they happen to have at the market but, like always, when you're cooking *Stella Style,* it's up to you! My three favorite mushrooms are portobello, oyster, and shiitake. They're almost always available at grocery stores these days. I also use creminis, sometimes known as baby portobellos, and enokis, which are great for accenting a salad or sauce. Once you get them home from the market, clean the mushrooms by wiping them with a damp cloth or using a mushroom brush. Rinsing or soaking them will cause them to absorb too much water and become spongy.

HELPFUL HINT

When you're grilling or having a party where you want finger foods, thread the whole mushrooms on skewers, grill them, and top with melted scampi butter!

"If You Had Wings" Chicken Wings

If you had wings to fly, you'd take to the skies as fast as you could to get to this mouthwatering appetizer! They're named after a ride at Disney World called "If You Had Wings." Back in the good old days, it was one of my favorites because it didn't take an expensive "E" ticket—plus you could get on fast! Anyway, if you love chicken wings the way we do, then this recipe is just the ("E") ticket!

3 to 6 cups vegetable oil (more or less depending on the pot used)
2 pounds or more fresh chicken wings, wing tips removed and discarded
Blackening Spice (page 90)

YIELD:
4 servings

NET CARBOHYDRATES:
0 grams per serving

PREP:
10 minutes

COOK:
8 to 10 minutes

1. Place a deep, heavy pot over medium-high heat and fill with at least 2 inches oil. Heat the oil to 375° F. (Portable deep fryers are great for this, but if you don't have one, you can use a candy thermometer—just be careful!)

2. Coat the chicken wings liberally with the blackening spice, then rub it in well with your hands.

3. Carefully drop the seasoned wings into the hot oil—use a slotted spoon and wear mitts—and fry until golden crispy brown, 8 to 10 minutes. Remove and drain the wings on paper towels.

HELPFUL HINTS

If you toss these wings in equal parts melted butter and Louisiana hot sauce, you can make Hot Wings—with zero carbs! If you want to cut down on fat, simply bake the wings instead of frying. Place them on a baking sheet with edges sprayed with vegetable oil cooking spray and bake at 400° F for about 50 minutes, until browned and tender.

Jimi's Fried Mozzarella Sticks

Jimi Volpe and I have been best friends for over thirty years. I was only fourteen and he was only fifteen when we worked together for the first time. Jimi was already cooking by then, and I was just a dishwasher. He took me under his wing, taught me how to cook the line, and the rest is history! Ten years later, Jimi and I were still working together, and that's when he taught me how to make these crowd-pleasing mozzarella sticks. I have only switched one ingredient—the soy flour in the breading—so they still taste exactly like the ones we made in the old days!

YIELD:
8 servings

NET CARBOHYDRATES:
5 grams per serving

PREP:
20 minutes

FREEZE:
2 hours

COOK:
about 2 minutes

3 to 6 cups vegetable oil (more or less depending on the pot used)
3 large eggs
¼ cup heavy cream or water

BREADING:
2⅓ cups soy flour
2 teaspoons salt
1 teaspoon freshly ground black pepper
1 teaspoon garlic powder
1 teaspoon poultry seasoning

12 mozzarella sticks, approximately 1 ounce each (we use the individually wrapped ones), or 12 ounces mozzarella

1. Place a deep, heavy pot over medium-high heat and fill with at least 2 inches oil. Heat the oil to 350° F. It's very important to monitor and maintain the temperature, or the breading and oil will burn. (Portable deep fryers are great for this, but if you don't have one, you can just a candy thermometer—just be careful!)

2. In a medium bowl, mix the eggs and cream to make an egg wash.

3. In a larger bowl, mix all the breading ingredients together.

4. Split the 12 mozzarella sticks directly down the center lengthwise, creating 24 "half" sticks total. (Otherwise they will be too large when breaded.) If you're cutting your own sticks, make 24 sticks that are about 3 inches long and $\frac{1}{2}$-inch wide.

5. Dip the mozzarella sticks first in the egg wash, then coat with the breading. Then repeat the process, dipping the sticks back into the egg wash and then the breading to be sure they're completely coated.

6. Pat off any excess breading and place the sticks in single layers on a small baking sheet that fits in your freezer. Use waxed paper between the layers so they don't stick together. Wrap and freeze them completely, about 2 hours, before frying. (This helps the breading fry into a crisp shell before the cheese has a chance to melt.)

7. Carefully place 3 or 4 of the frozen breaded mozzarella sticks at a time into the hot oil—use a slotted spoon and wear mitts—and fry until golden crispy brown, about 2 minutes. Don't leave them in too long or the cheese will melt and ooze out of the breading shell. Repeat with remaining sticks. Remove from the oil and drain on paper towels. Serve hot with our Marinara Sauce (page 58) or Horseradish Creamy Sauce (page 85).

HELPFUL HINT

If you have any breading left over, don't throw it out. Sift it with a wire-mesh strainer, put it in a sealed container, and keep it in your freezer until next time!

Teriyaki Ginger Garlic Chicken Satay

Our boys just love Asian food, and this recipe's at the top of their list! Chicken thighs are moister than lean breast, and Rachel loves that we can usually find chicken thighs on sale! This recipe will get the party started right or make an excellent main course. It even makes enough for you to sneak a few in the kitchen before serving!

YIELD:
24 servings

NET CARBOHYDRATES:
0 grams per serving

PREP:
30 minutes

MARINATE:
1 hour

COOK:
20 minutes

MARINADE:
15 ounces teriyaki sauce (no more than 2 grams sugar
    per serving)
6 tablespoons sesame oil
1 teaspoon minced fresh garlic
1 tablespoon minced fresh ginger
Juice of 1 lemon
1 tablespoon sugar substitute (Splenda recommended)

2 pounds boneless, skinless chicken thighs
1 tablespoon sesame seeds, toasted*

Special equipment: Twenty-four 8-inch bamboo skewers

1. Mix all the marinade ingredients together in a nonreactive container large enough to hold all of the chicken.

2. Cut the chicken into twenty-four ¹/₂-inch-wide strips. Add to the marinade, cover, shake gently to mix, and refrigerate for at least 1 hour.

3. Soak the bamboo skewers in water for 30 minutes to keep them from burning later.

4. Preheat the oven to 375° F.

5. Thread 1 chicken strip onto each skewer, leaving about an inch of bamboo free at the blunt end, and line up on a baking sheet. Place in the oven and bake for about 20 minutes, until fully cooked through. Sprinkle the skewers with toasted sesame seeds before serving.

*COOK'S TIP: To toast sesame seeds, heat a small skillet until hot. Add the raw seeds and stir gently with a wooden spoon until they brown and begin to pop. Remove from the heat and let cool.

HELPFUL HINT

For a more dramatic presentation, cut a cantaloupe in half, hollow it with a melon baller, and place it on a platter as if were a bowl. Fill it up with the melon balls, then stick the skewers around the rim of the cantaloupe bowl.

Condiments, Spices, and Dressings

s any good cook knows, even an inexpensive cut of meat can taste like sirloin with the right mix of spices or sauces. However, as you'll recall from carb-proofing your pantry, many store-bought condiments are just loaded with sugar. Don't forget that when we say sugar we mean corn syrup too! But that doesn't mean you have to make do without your favorite condiments—far from it! I'd never ask you to give up ketchup on your hot dog or hamburger. Just enjoy them with one of our *Stella Style* classics—**Quick and Easy Ketchup**!

In this section, we'll introduce you to low-carb **Blackening Spice**, **Horseradish Cream Sauce**, and **No-Cook Bourbon Barbecue Sauce**. For seafood there's **Cocktail Sauce** and **Scampi Butter**, and who wouldn't love some **Cranberry Relish** for their holiday turkey? For authentic low-carb Mexican food, don't forget my **Pico de Gallo** and my low-carb **Guacamole** (page 63)! And if you're in the mood for a salad, then check out my low-carb **Thousand Island Dressing** or Rachel's classic **Greek Dressing**.

With *Stella Style*, spice is the variety of life!

Wild Mushroom Turkey Gravy

Quick and Easy Ketchup

Mustard Sauce

Sweet Mustard Sauce

Horseradish Cream Sauce

Cocktail Sauce

Remoulade Sauce

Scampi Butter

No-Cook Bourbon Barbecue Sauce

Blackening Spice

Pico de Gallo

Cranberry Relish

Thousand Island Dressing

Greek Dressing

Wild Mushroom Turkey Gravy

Here's the perfect way to use those juices and drippings from your next roasted turkey. There's more than one way to thicken a sauce or gravy! Since flour and cornstarch are out when you're eating low-carb, a classic French cream reduction is in order. This rich sauce is complemented by the hearty taste of the mushrooms, and it's a great accompaniment to anyone's Thanksgiving turkey!

YIELD:
12 servings

NET CARBOHYDRATES:
2 grams per serving

PREP:
10 minutes

COOK:
15 minutes

2 cups turkey juices and drippings from roasting pan
½ cup heavy cream
3 tablespoons unsalted butter
10 ounces mushrooms, stemmed and sliced (we like shiitake, but any mushroom is fine)
1 tablespoon chopped fresh thyme
⅛ teaspoon minced fresh garlic
¼ cup dry sherry
Salt and freshly ground black pepper

1. Collect the turkey juices from the roasting pan. Remove the fat either by using a fat separator or by refrigerating the juices and skimming off the fat that rises to the top. Discard the fat.

2. Transfer the juices to a small saucepan, bring to a simmer over medium-high heat, and cook until reduced by half.

3. Add the cream. Continue to cook until the gravy is thick enough to coat the back of a spoon, about 8 minutes.

4. Heat the butter in a separate pan. Add the mushrooms, thyme, garlic, and sherry and sauté over medium-high heat until tender.

5. Combine the sautéed mushrooms with the reduced gravy.

6. Finish by seasoning with salt and pepper to taste. Transfer to a gravy boat and keep warm until serving.

HELPFUL HINT

If the sauce is too thin, simply continue to reduce it until you achieve the thickness you desire. Stirring in a pat of butter just before serving will do wonders for the flavor!

Quick and Easy Ketchup

Our family couldn't live without ketchup, so one of the first things we had to reinvent was a quick and easy ketchup. Nothing fancy, but it sure does the trick, and without all those corn syrup solids you get with the store-bought variety. And did I mention that it's EASY? Believe me, when you want ketchup on that burger or hot dog, you're going to be grateful you spent a few minutes to make this up. Enjoy it in moderation, since it does have natural sugars from the tomatoes.

YIELD:
24 servings;
2 tablespoons per
serving

NET CARBOHYDRATES:
1 gram per serving

PREP:
5 minutes

8 ounces sugar-free tomato sauce
6 ounces sugar-free tomato paste
2 tablespoons white vinegar
¼ cup sugar substitute (Splenda recommended)

1. Mix all ingredients together in a small bowl. Refrigerate until ready to serve. Store any leftovers in an airtight container in the refrigerator; the ketchup will stay fresh for about a week.

HELPFUL HINT

I like homemade condiments because they're fresh and don't have sugar. However, they also have no preservatives, which is why they only last about a week if properly stored and refrigerated.

Mustard Sauce

As a chef in Florida, I used to serve this mustard sauce with stone crab claws. It's not only carb-free, but it also brings out the flavor of so many different foods. We use it on cold cuts like roast beef, turkey, and ham, and it's a must for burgers. It's especially good with my Key West Crab Cakes (page 146)! Easy to make, it's a great alternative to ketchup!

¼ **cup mayonnaise**
¼ **cup Dijon mustard**
¼ **teaspoon fresh lemon juice**

1. Mix all ingredients together in a small bowl. Cover and refrigerate until ready to serve.

HELPFUL HINT

Keep this in an airtight container in the refrigerator up to a week.

> YIELD:
> 12 servings,
> 1 tablespoon per
> serving
>
> NET CARBOHYDRATES:
> 0 grams per serving
>
> PREP:
> 5 minutes

Sweet Mustard Sauce

This is a great substitute for honey mustard sauce, which is normally laden with sugars. Try it with chicken fingers or my Teriyaki Chicken Satay (page 76). I like it as a dip, too, for rolled-up lunch meats like turkey, ham, and roast beef!

YIELD:
8 servings, 1 tablespoon per serving

NET CARBOHYDRATES:
1 gram per serving

PREP:
5 minutes

¼ cup mayonnaise
¼ cup yellow table mustard
2 tablespoons sugar substitute (Splenda recommended)
1 teaspoon brown sugar substitute, optional (we use Sugar Twin Brown Sugar Replacement, but it's difficult to find)

1. Mix all the ingredients in a bowl until blended. Store any leftovers in a covered plastic or glass container. This sauce will keep fresh for 1 week if refrigerated.

HELPFUL HINT

Try using this as a glaze for baked ham or even baked chicken breast!

Horseradish Cream Sauce

It's come to the point where I can hardly eat prime rib without horseradish cream sauce. Fortunately, this sauce is naturally low-carb; I've been making this one for over twenty-five years! It's also great as a dip for fried foods, like Jimi's Fried Mozzarella Sticks (page 74), and Deep-Fried Onion Rings (page 188).

$\frac{1}{2}$ **cup sour cream**
$\frac{1}{2}$ **cup mayonnaise**
2 to 3 tablespoons prepared red or white horseradish,
    (you can use more or less to taste)
1 teaspoon fresh lemon juice

1. Put all the ingredients into a bowl and mix until completely blended. This sauce will keep for 1 week when refrigerated in a covered plastic or glass container.

YIELD:
8 servings,
2 tablespoons each

NET CARBOHYDRATES:
0 carbs per serving

PREP:
10 minutes

Cocktail Sauce

Store-bought cocktail sauce is almost always made with a ton of sugar. Our version is a great low-carb condiment with only natural sugars derived from the tomato products, which, when eaten in moderation, are just fine for eating *Stella Style*.

YIELD:
24 servings,
1 tablespoon each

NET CARBOHYDRATES:
1 gram per serving

PREP:
5 minutes

½ **cup sugar-free tomato sauce**

½ **cup chili sauce (or additional sugar-free tomato sauce)**

¾ **cup sugar-free tomato paste**

¼ **cup red or white horseradish (you can use more or less to taste)**

2 **tablespoons white vinegar**

1 **tablespoon fresh lemon juice**

¼ **cup sugar substitute (Splenda recommended)**

1. Mix all ingredients together in a small bowl. This sauce for will stay fresh for 1 week when refrigerated in a plastic or glass container.

HELPFUL HINT

Try this sauce with Jimi's Fried Mozzarella Sticks (page 74) or as a dip for shrimp, crab legs, or other shellfish.

Remoulade Sauce

I've always been a big fan of Cajun cooking, and this is a sauce that just screams New Orleans! It's the perfect spicy accompaniment for everything from seafood to steaks, even deli meats!

1 cup mayonnaise
2 tablespoons fresh lemon juice
1 tablespoons Blackening Spice (page 90)
1 tablespoon sugar-free tomato paste
1 tablespoon whole-grain Dijon mustard
½ teaspoon Tabasco sauce
½ teaspoon Worcestershire sauce
Salt and freshly ground black pepper to taste

YIELD:
24 servings,
1 teaspoon each

NET CARBOHYDRATES:
0 grams

PREP:
5 minutes

1. Place all ingredients in a bowl and mix well with a whisk. Store in a covered plastic or glass container. The sauce will keep fresh refrigerated for 4 to 5 days.

HELPFUL HINT

This sauce is exceptionally good with my Key West Crab Cakes (page 146) or with my Blackened Sea Scallops (page 142).

Scampi Butter

The reason chefs make compound butters ahead of time and then tuck them into the refrigerator is that we can store so many of the ingredients we need for certain gourmet meals in one convenient place—the butter. This really saves a lot of time, especially when you need to put a meal together in just a few minutes (like during Saturday night dinner rush at a busy restaurant). At home, the practice is just as useful. Try this Scampi Butter for seasoning almost anything—*Stella Style!*

YIELD:
12 servings,
1 tablespoon per
serving

NET CARBS:
0 grams per serving

PREP:
15 minutes

½ cup (1 stick) unsalted butter, softened
1 tablespoon minced fresh garlic
2 tablespoons minced red onion
1 tablespoon chopped fresh parsley leaves
½ teaspoon garlic powder
1 tablespoon kosher salt
¼ teaspoon freshly ground black pepper
Dash of ground white pepper
Dash of Worcestershire sauce
Juice of 1 lemon

1. In a bowl, whisk together all ingredients until well blended. It takes a bit of work, but if you keep whisking, it will mix together. (If you have trouble getting the liquid to combine, it may help to soften the butter in the microwave for just a couple seconds.)

2. Spoon the compound butter onto a piece of plastic wrap and form it into a log about 2 inches around. Roll it up like a big cigar and twist the ends shut. You may store the butter in the refrigerator for 1 week or freeze for much longer.

HELPFUL HINT

Reduce the garlic by half in this recipe and add 2 tablespoons of any chopped fresh herb for a completely different compound butter.

No-Cook Bourbon Barbecue Sauce

This sauce is surprisingly simple to prepare because it's full of chef's shortcuts. You get a gourmet result with half the effort! And, of course, the old saying applies here: If you make it yourself, you know what's in it!

One 29-ounce can sugar-free tomato sauce
One 6-ounce can sugar-free tomato paste
2 ounces bourbon
2 tablespoons white vinegar
2 tablespoons liquid smoke
1 tablespoon Worcestershire sauce
1½ teaspoons hot sauce
¾ cup sugar substitute (Splenda recommended)
¼ cup brown sugar substitute, optional
    (Sugar Twin recommended)
2 tablespoons finely chopped red onion
1 small clove garlic, minced
¼ teaspoon garlic powder
1 tablespoon kosher salt
1 teaspoon freshly ground black pepper
1 teaspoon onion powder

> **YIELD:**
> 32 servings,
> 2 tablespoons each
>
> **NET CARBOHYDRATES:**
> 2 grams per serving
>
> **PREP:**
> 15 minutes

1. Put all ingredients into a bowl and whisk well to combine. Store in an airtight container and refrigerate. The sauce will stay fresh for about a week.

HELPFUL HINT

This sauce is great for all barbecue recipes from ribs to chicken, and it also makes a great dip for fried foods like chicken tenders.

Blackening Spice

This has got to be one of the most versatile and valuable spices in our kitchen! Back in the early '80s, Paul Prudhomme gave me some tips about blackening techniques and Cajun seasonings that I've been using ever since. You can use this seasoning mix to blacken everything from chicken and fish to pork chops and steaks. We even season our vegetables with it! And, most importantly, it makes a great alternative to store-bought seasonings, which are usually full of sugars and fillers!

YIELD:
about 1 cup

NET CARBOHYDRATES:
0 grams

PREP:
10 minutes

5 tablespoons kosher salt
5 tablespoons paprika
1 tablespoon dried thyme
1 tablespoon freshly ground black pepper
1 tablespoon garlic powder
½ teaspoon cayenne pepper
½ teaspoon ground white pepper

1. Mix all the ingredients well and store in an airtight container or spice canister.

HELPFUL HINT

We always keep this around in the kitchen and use it for everything from pork chops to grilled vegetables. You can use it for pan-fried, grilled, or even baked foods—just shake it on until all surfaces are well-covered—and then add a little more!

Pico de Gallo

I was going to "pico" a different name for this one—maybe something like "salsa"—but since we chefs like flair so much, I'm sticking with the original. You can use this popular, naturally low-carb, spicy Mexican staple to light up many of your favorite meals. But don't use too much, or your tongue may flare up!

4 Roma tomatoes, seeded and diced
¼ cup diced red onion
¼ cup diced red bell pepper
¼ cup diced green bell pepper
1 teaspoon minced fresh jalapeño pepper, without seeds
1 small clove garlic, minced
1 tablespoon finely chopped fresh cilantro
1 teaspoon fresh lime juice
2 dashes hot sauce (we use Tabasco; you may also
    use ½ teaspoon cayenne pepper)
Salt and freshly ground black pepper to taste

YIELD:
12 servings,
2 tablespoons each

NET CARBOHYDRATES:
2 grams per serving

PREP:
10 minutes

1. Mix all ingredients together well in a nonreactive bowl and chill before serving.

2. Refrigerate any leftovers in a covered nonreactive container. It will stay fresh in your refrigerator for about a week.

HELPFUL HINT

Pico de Gallo is even better the next day when the flavors have had a chance to meld. It's the perfect accompaniment for Three-Cheese Veggie Quesadillas (page 154), Ginny's Taco Salad (page 171), or even to top the Chili Turkey Burgers (page 134)!

Cranberry Relish

Cranberries are a must-have for certain holiday dinners. Lucky for us, they're naturally low in carbs. Unfortunately, almost all the cranberry relishes and sauces you'll find in your market are full of sugar! This relish is all about the cranberries, and since you'll be making it fresh, it'll taste better than the store-bought versions—and without all that unnecessary sugar!

YIELD:
12 servings

NET CARBOHYDRATES:
3 grams per serving

PREP:
5 minutes

COOK:
15 minutes

1 cup sugar substitute (Splenda recommended)
1 cup water
12 ounces cranberries, fresh or frozen
1 teaspoon freshly grated orange zest

1. Combine the sugar substitute and water in a saucepan and bring to a boil.

2. Add the cranberries and orange zest and bring back to a boil. Reduce the heat to low and simmer for 10 minutes, stirring occasionally.

3. Remove from the heat, cool, cover, and refrigerate until serving.

HELPFUL HINT

Before cooking, rinse the cranberries and pick through them to remove any rotten berries and stems.

Thousand Island Dressing

Most store-bought dressings are made with sugar, and Thousand Island is no exception. We like it so much, however, that we reinvented it as soon as we started low-carbing. Made with sugar-free ketchup and relish, it can be eaten it to your heart's content!

½ cup mayonnaise
2 tablespoons Quick and Easy Ketchup (page 82)
1 tablespoon white vinegar
1 tablespoon sugar substitute (Splenda recommended)
1 tablespoon sugar-free sweet pickle relish
　　(we use Mt. Olive brand)
1 teaspoon minced red onion
⅛ teaspoon salt
⅛ teaspoon freshly ground black pepper

YIELD:
6 servings

NET CARBOHYDRATES:
1 gram per serving

PREP:
15 minutes

COOK:
5 minutes

1. Thoroughly combine all of the ingredients in a bowl. Store any leftovers in a covered container. This dressing keeps for 1 week when refrigerated.

HELPFUL HINT

Add a dash of brandy and ¼ teaspoon minced fresh garlic for a flavorful alternative!

Greek Dressing

I asked Rachel whether I'd forgotten to include any important recipes in this book, and she immediately said "Greek Salad." A few minutes later she tossed me a crumpled piece of paper, covered in scribbles, and said this was her favorite way to make the dressing. (It all looked like Greek to me!) It took some deciphering, but here it is (I think).

<table>
<tr><td>

YIELD:
4 servings

NET CARBOHYDRATES:
1 gram per serving

PREP:
15 minutes

</td><td>

1 teaspoon Dijon mustard
¼ cup red wine vinegar
2 tablespoons white wine vinegar
1 clove garlic, peeled
1 teaspoon salt, plus additional to taste
½ teaspoon freshly ground black pepper
¼ teaspoon crushed red pepper flakes, optional; you may substitute a dash of cayenne pepper
⅓ cup extra-virgin olive oil
½ cup canola oil
1 teaspoon dried oregano or Italian seasoning blend

</td></tr>
</table>

1. In a blender or food processor, mix the mustard, vinegars, garlic, salt, and black and red peppers until completely blended.

2. With the machine on, very slowly pour in the olive oil in a continuous steady stream, then pour in the canola oil the same way.

3. Pour the dressing into a small bowl and stir in the oregano. Add salt to taste. The dressing will keep for 2 weeks in the refrigerator in a covered glass container.

HELPFUL HINT

Try this dressing on Rachel's favorite, Ernie's Greek Salad (page 167). And be sure to make more than you need. The flavors really blend after a day or two—so it will be even better then!

Anytime Entrées

**tella Style** is all about breaking the rules of eating—the rules, that is, that tell you what to eat and when to eat it. You'll find a recipe for a terrific omelet under **Morning Starters**, but who says an omelet is only for breakfast? Why can't you have one for lunch, say, or for dinner? Why can't you start the morning with **Key West Crab Cakes**, or a slice of last night's **Roasted Rosemary Pork Loin** alongside an egg over easy? Or why not surprise everyone at the dinner table with a **Greek Salad**!

The point is, **Anytime Entrées** mean just what they say. You can—and should—enjoy **meats, poultry, fish and seafood, salads and soups, and vegetarian entrées** any time of the day.

We all get into the habit of eating the same things at the same time every day of the week. (If you're like the old me, for instance, breakfast is always toast, cereal, and a glass of juice; lunch is always a sandwich, a piece of fruit, and some chips; dinner is always meat and potatoes!) This is one of the reasons it's so hard to make changes in the way you eat. If you want to break your dependence on high-carbohydrate foods, you've also got to break the rules about **when** you eat certain foods. It won't happen overnight, but once you open your mind to the possibilities, you'll find it easier and easier to reach for the right foods—anytime!

Meats

I usually have to spend so much time trying to convince people that eating low-carb doesn't necessarily mean eating meat morning, noon, and night, that it's nice to finally have the chance to say a few good things about it! Beef and pork are great sources of protein, they can be prepared in hundreds of different ways, and they keep and travel well after you've cooked them. And while you do need to think a few hours ahead when you're making a baked ham, you can have a steak on and off the grill in fewer than 15 minutes! So take a look at this sampling of recipes—and don't forget to put the leftovers to good use the day after!

If you think your days of chili and lasagna are over, think again! With our **Black Soy Bean Chili**, soybeans stand in for their high-carb cousin, kidney beans. And with *Stella Style Meat Lasagna*, you'll never miss the noodles!

You'll find some party showstoppers here. Try serving **Grilled Country-Style Pork Ribs with Bourbon Barbecue Sauce**, **Gorgonzola Beef Tenderloin**, or **Tequila-Marinated Pork Loin** at your next get-together. Then sit back and wait for the applause!

Black Soy Bean Chili

Corned Beef and Cabbage

Stuffed Meat Loaf Rollatini

Stuffed Cabbage

Gram's Stuffed Eggplant

Claire's Stuffed Pumpkin

Stuffed Peppers

Foolproof Roast Beef

Gorgonzola Beef Tenderloin

Meat Lasagna

Mock Fettuccine Carbonara

Baked Ham with Maple Bourbon Glaze

Grilled Country-Style Pork Ribs with Bourbon Barbecue Sauce

Anthony's Pork Chops Parmesan

Roasted Rosemary Pork Loin

Tequila-Marinated Grilled Boneless Pork Loin

Black Soy Bean Chili

Everything in ordinary chili—except the beans—is naturally low-carb. Therefore, if you use soybeans, which are available in most health food stores these days, you can follow a low-carb lifestyle and still enjoy this Southwestern favorite. Black soy beans are not only full of fiber but also taste great in this quick-and-easy ground beef chili!

YIELD:
8 servings

NET CARBOHYDRATES:
4 grams per serving

PREP:
15 minutes

COOK:
18 minutes

2 tablespoons vegetable oil

1 green bell pepper, cut into large dice

1 red bell pepper, cut into large dice

½ cup chopped red onion

2½ pounds ground chuck (you may use any cut of beef you like)

¼ cup chili powder

3 tablespoons ground cumin

1 teaspoon minced fresh garlic

2 teaspoons kosher salt

1 teaspoon freshly ground black pepper

½ teaspoon garlic powder

¼ teaspoon cayenne pepper

3 Roma tomatoes, diced

One 15-ounce can black soy beans, drained and rinsed

2 tablespoons chopped fresh cilantro

1. Heat the oil in a large skillet over medium-high heat. Add the peppers and onion and cook until slightly tender.

2. Add the ground beef and spices and cook until the meat is thoroughly browned. Drain off the excess fat using a spoon or turkey baster.

3. Add the diced tomatoes and beans and simmer for about 10 minutes, stirring occasionally.

4. To serve, garnish the chili with cilantro.

HELPFUL HINTS

Feel free to garnish the chili with my favorite low-carb toppings: shredded Monterey Jack or Cheddar cheese, a dollop of sour cream, or sliced green onion tops (scallions). Freeze the leftovers for a great anytime meal, or simply put the cold chili on top of a salad with cheese.

Corned Beef and Cabbage

This dinner is a favorite of Rachel's to make and a favorite of mine to eat. Even though we come from different backgrounds and were raised in different parts of the country, Rachel and I have discovered that we ate a lot of the same foods growing up. This recipe is a good example—both of our mothers made it exactly the same way. Today you can find this easy, boiled dinner on our table all the time, but especially on St. Patrick's Day!

YIELD:
8 servings

NET CARBOHYDRATES:
3 grams per serving

PREP:
15 minutes

COOK:
approximately
3¼ hours

One 4-pound corned beef brisket
3 tablespoons pickling spice (put it inside a tea ball if you don't want the spices to remain in the dish
4 ribs celery, cut into 3-inch pieces
1 small rutabaga, cut into 1-inch squares, optional
1 head green cabbage, cored and cut into 8 wedges

1. Fill a large pot halfway with water and place it over high heat.

2. Add the corned beef and pickling spice to the pot and bring the water to a boil.

3. Lower the temperature until the water is simmering, then cook for about 3 hours, until the meat is so tender it tears with a fork.

4. Take the corned beef out of the water but don't discard the water. Let the corned beef rest for 15 minutes before thinly slicing against the grain of the meat.

5. While the meat is resting, turn the temperature up just a bit under the water and add the celery, rutabaga if using, and cabbage. Cook for about 15 minutes, until tender.

6. Serve a little bit of everything on each plate and make sure it's "boiling hot!"

HELPFUL HINTS

I like to melt a pat of butter over everything on the plate, and Rachel likes to mash the rutabaga. You can never have too much corned beef, since it makes a great zero-carb deli meat for the next couple days! Try it with Thousand Island Dressing (page 93) wrapped in lettuce.

Stuffed Meat Loaf Rollatini

I'm one of those people who could eat meat loaf cold for breakfast. Wait a minute. I *do* eat cold meat loaf for breakfast, and I love it! I learned how to make meat loaf from my mother, who loved it as well. Meat loaf is such a versatile recipe, and this stuffed meat loaf can be made many, many ways without changing anything but the filling. Yet with every change, it tastes like a whole new meal! This is everyone's favorite at our house! How will you make it?

YIELD:
8 servings

NET CARBOHYDRATES:
6 grams per serving

PREP:
30 minutes

COOK:
1¼ hours

2 pounds ground chuck (you may use meat loaf mix*)
2 large eggs
½ cup grated Parmesan cheese
¼ cup finely diced red onion
¼ cup diced roasted or fresh red bell pepper
2 tablespoons chopped fresh parsley
2 cloves garlic, minced
½ teaspoon dried oregano
½ teaspoon dried basil
1 teaspoon kosher salt
½ teaspoon freshly ground black pepper
4 ounces baked ham, thinly sliced
8 ounces mozzarella cheese, sliced or shredded
1 cup Quick and Easy Ketchup (page 82), optional

Special equipment: 9 x 5-inch loaf pan

1. Preheat the oven to 350° F.

2. In a large bowl, mix together the beef, eggs, Parmesan, onion, peppers, parsley, garlic, herbs, and seasonings.

3. Spread a piece of waxed paper on the counter or a baking sheet. Place the meat mixture on the waxed paper and form it into a 10 x 8-inch rectangle.

4. Place the ham in a layer on top of the meat and follow it with a layer of cheese.

5. Beginning with the short end, roll up the stuffed meat loaf mix like a jellyroll and seal the edges all around by pinching the meat. Place the roll, seam side down, in the loaf pan.

6. If desired, spread a heavy coat of ketchup over the top of the meat loaf.

7. Bake for about 1¼ hours, until a meat thermometer registers 165° F. Drain off the fat and let the meat loaf rest at least 10 minutes before cutting into 8 slices.

*COOK'S TIP: Feel free to use your supermarket's meat loaf mix, which may be a combination of pork, veal, and beef, or you can substitute ground turkey or chicken for any or all of the ground chuck.

HELPFUL HINT

Try stuffing this meat loaf with pepperoni in place of the ham. Or try bacon and American cheese, or Swiss cheese and mushrooms, or even spinach and ricotta cheese!

Stuffed Cabbage

This recipe is the one my mother used to make stuffed cabbage, and if you've already tried her meat loaf recipe, you may see a pattern forming. That's right, it's all about the toppings! Here you've still got the ketchup topping—which is a signature of my mother's cooking—but without the sugar! So stuff yourself—*Stella Style!*

YIELD:
6 servings

NET CARBOHYDRATES:
2 grams per serving

PREP:
30 minutes

COOK:
45 to 50 minutes

1 head green cabbage

MEAT STUFFING:
2 pounds ground beef
¼ cup diced green bell pepper
¼ cup diced onion
¼ teaspoon minced fresh garlic
2 large eggs
2 teaspoons salt
1 teaspoon freshly ground black pepper

6 tablespoons Quick and Easy Ketchup (page 82)
2 tablespoons diced green bell pepper

1. Preheat the oven to 375° F.

2. Fill a large pot halfway with water and bring to a slow boil over high heat.

3. Carefully cut off the bottom of the cabbage and remove as much of the core as possible while leaving the head intact. Drop the whole cabbage carefully into the boiling water. In just a minute the leaves will start to come loose. Using tongs or a fork, pull the loose leaves out of the water and set them aside. Work quickly so the leaves don't overcook. (You need 12 to 15 leaves for this recipe.) Take the remainder of the cabbage out of the water and save it for another meal.

4. Mix the meat stuffing ingredients together in a bowl.

5. Place a small amount of meat stuffing in a single cabbage leaf and roll it up like a cigar, making sure to tuck in the ends first. (You may make the cabbage rolls any size you like. Mine are usually the size of D-cell batteries.)

6. Place the stuffed cabbage rolls in a single layer in a shallow baking dish. Cover with the ketchup, then sprinkle with the diced green pepper.

7. Cover the dish tightly with aluminum foil and bake for about 45 minutes, until cooked through. Serve hot. (Be careful when you remove the foil because the escaping steam can burn you.)

HELPFUL HINTS

This is a great meal to freeze in individual portions for anytime, anywhere meals! The leftover cabbage can be sautéed as a dinner vegetable or used in a stir-fry.

Gram's Stuffed Eggplant

I was five or six years old when my grandmother gave me my first plate of this eggplant. When she said it was called eggplant, all I could think of was how strange it was that eggs were growing on plants! I've loved eggplant ever since and have learned to cook it in many different ways, but I always go back to my grandmother's favorite eggplant recipe!

YIELD:
4 servings

NET CARBOHYDRATES:
3 grams per serving

PREP:
15 minutes

COOK:
30 minutes

Vegetable oil cooking spray

2 tablespoons olive oil

½ cup diced red bell pepper

¼ cup diced red onion

½ teaspoon minced fresh garlic

1½ pounds ground chuck (fattier cuts work better, but you may buy lean if you like)

1 cup shredded mozzarella cheese

¼ cup grated Parmesan cheese

1 large egg

1 tablespoon chopped fresh Italian parsley, plus additional for garnish

1 teaspoon kosher salt

½ teaspoon freshly ground black pepper

½ teaspoon dried basil

½ teaspoon dried oregano

¼ teaspoon garlic powder

2 medium eggplants

1. Preheat the oven to 350° F. Spray a baking dish with vegetable oil cooking spray and set aside.

2. Heat the olive oil in a skillet over medium-high heat. Add the pepper, onion, and garlic and sauté until tender. Remove from the heat and transfer to a bowl.

3. Add the remaining ingredients except for the eggplant to the bowl, reserving a small handful of mozzarella for topping. Mix well.

4. Cut the eggplant lengthwise in half and use a spoon to scrape out a little of the center to make room for the stuffing. Be careful not to dig too deep or you will scrape through the bottom of the eggplant. Pile the stuffing high on each of the eggplant halves.

5. Place the eggplants in the baking dish and bake for about 30 minutes, until the stuffing is fully cooked and tender.

6. Remove from the oven and immediately sprinkle with the reserved mozzarella.

7. Garnish with parsley and serve.

HELPFUL HINT

You can stuff zucchini or yellow squash the same way!

Claire's Stuffed Pumpkin

While growing up in Woonsocket, Rhode Island, Rachel's mother Claire learned to make this stuffed pumpkin, and now it's become one of our favorites as well! It's wonderful to see a beloved dish like this one pass from one family to another. Given the way Anthony and Christian took to it, I have a feeling they'll keep the tradition alive!

YIELD:
6 servings

NET CARBOHYDRATES:
4 grams per serving

PREP:
20 minutes

COOK:
1½ hours

2 tablespoons vegetable oil
½ cup chopped onion
1½ cup chopped celery
1 pound ground beef
8 ounces ground pork
1 teaspoon salt
½ teaspoon freshly ground black pepper
1½ teaspoons garlic powder
¼ cup beef stock
1½ teaspoons ground cloves
1½ teaspoons ground cinnamon
1½ teaspoons pumpkin pie spice
2 tablespoons brandy
One 2 to 2½-pound pie pumpkin (also called a sugar pumpkin, this is smaller and sweeter than a carving pumpkin)
¼ cup brown sugar substitute (Brown Sugar Twin or any other)
¼ cup sugar substitute (Splenda recommended)

1. Preheat the oven to 350° F.

2. In a large sauté pan, heat the vegetable oil over medium-high heat. Add the onion and celery and cook until tender. Remove and set the vegetables aside.

3. Place the same pan over high heat. Add the ground beef, pork, salt, pepper, and garlic powder and cook until the meat is thoroughly browned. Drain off the excess fat using a spoon or turkey baster.

4. Turn the heat off and stir the sautéed veggies, beef stock, cloves, cinnamon, pumpkin pie spice, and brandy into the meat mixture.

5. Prepare the pumpkin as you would for Halloween: Cut off the top and set it aside for later. Scoop out the stringy fiber and seeds and discard. Mix the sugar substitutes together and sprinkle inside the cleaned pumpkin.

6. Fill the pumpkin with the cooked meat mixture and replace the top.

7. Bake in a shallow pan for about 1½ hours, until the pumpkin is tender when stuck with a fork. Remove the pumpkin from the oven, take off the top, cut into 6 wedges, and serve the pumpkin and meat together.

COOK'S TIP: Are you a fan of pumpkin seeds? Separate them from the fiber, rinse them thoroughly, spread them on a baking sheet, sprinkle with salt, and bake at 350° F for 15 to 20 minutes, until crisp. With only 5 net carbs per ¼ cup, pumpkin seeds are a fabulous snack *Stella Style.*

Stuffed Peppers

Stuffed foods are easy to make and exceptionally satisfying probably because of the wonderful combinations of tastes and textures! From Gram's Stuffed Eggplant (page 106) to Stuffed Cabbage (page 104) to these Stuffed Peppers, you can stuff yourself without guilt! Now that's what I call eating *Stella Style!*

YIELD:
6 servings

NET CARBOHYDRATES:
5 grams per serving

PREP:
20 minutes

COOK:
45 to 50 minutes

MEAT STUFFING:
2 pounds ground beef
$\frac{1}{2}$ cup diced onion
$\frac{1}{4}$ teaspoon minced fresh garlic
2 large eggs
2 teaspoons salt
1 teaspoon freshly ground black pepper

6 medium green bell peppers
6 tablespoons Quick and Easy Ketchup (page 82), optional

1. Preheat the oven to 375° F.

2. Put all the meat stuffing ingredients into a bowl and mix well.

3. Cut the tops off the peppers and clean out the seeds and ribs. Fill each pepper equally with the meat stuffing. (It's just fine if they're not full—or if they're overfull!)

4. Place the stuffed peppers in a single layer in a deep baking dish. Spoon 1 tablespoon of the ketchup over each pepper if desired.

5. Cover the dish tightly with aluminum foil and bake for about 45 minutes, until the peppers are cooked through. Serve hot. (Watch out for the steam when you take off the aluminum foil for it can burn!)

HELPFUL HINT

Rachel likes to make these using a mixture of 2 parts ground beef and 1 part ground pork. If you're watching your fat, you can replace the ground beef with ground turkey!

Foolproof Roast Beef

Cooking a roast beef slowly, at a low temperature, is the secret to making any cut of beef tender enough to melt in your mouth! This recipe is the same one professional chefs use. A cap of kosher salt seals in the juices and makes for a flavorful, tender roast every time!

**One 4-pound sirloin tip roast (you may use prime rib or
    a similar cut)**
1 tablespoon freshly ground black pepper
½ teaspoon minced fresh garlic
½ cup kosher salt

YIELD:
12 servings

NET CARBOHYDRATES:
0 grams per serving

PREP:
10 minutes

COOK:
4 to 5 hours

1. Preheat the oven to 210° F.

2. Place the roast fat side up in a shallow roasting pan.

3. Season the meat with the black pepper and garlic, then cover completely with a heavy layer (cap) of kosher salt.

4. Place the pan in the oven and roast for 4 to 5 hours, until a meat thermometer stuck in the thickest part of the beef registers 140° to 145° F if you like your meat rare. The thermometer should read 145° for medium rare, 160° for medium, and 170° for well done.

5. Remove the roast from the oven and let rest for at least 10 minutes. Remove the salt cap before cutting into 12 slices.

HELPFUL HINT

The leftovers are delicious sliced and served with Mustard Sauce (page 83).

Gorgonzola Beef Tenderloin

I apprenticed under French chefs as a young man, when it was customary to put blue cheese and butter on top of hot steak just before serving, so it would arrive melting at the table. Just the sight of it makes your mouth water! Here's my version of this delicious French classic—*Stella Style!*

YIELD:
3 servings

NET CARBOHYDRATES:
2 grams per serving

PREP:
20 minutes

COOK:
10 minutes

1 tablespoons canola oil
1 tablespoon unsalted butter
1 pound beef tenderloin, cut into 6 medallions
$\frac{1}{4}$ teaspoon kosher salt
$\frac{1}{4}$ teaspoon freshly ground black pepper
2 tablespoons chopped red onion
$\frac{1}{4}$ teaspoon minced fresh garlic
3 tablespoons red wine

GORGONZOLA SAUCE:
$\frac{2}{3}$ cup sour cream
$\frac{1}{3}$ cup mayonnaise
4 ounces Gorgonzola cheese, crumbled
$1\frac{1}{2}$ teaspoons Worcestershire sauce

1. Heat the oil and butter in a large sauté pan over high heat until almost smoking hot. (Using oil with the butter does wonders for the flavor, and the oil helps keep the butter from burning.)

2. Season both sides of the tenderloin medallions with salt and pepper, then add them to the hot pan.

3. Add the onion and garlic and continue to sear the first side of the beef for about 2 minutes.

4. Turn the medallions over, cook for about 1 minute more, then add the red wine.

5. Cook just until the liquid thickens, about 2 minutes more, and remove from the heat.

6. Make the Gorgonzola sauce: Combine the sour cream, mayonnaise, Gorgonzola, and Worcestershire in a saucepan. Cook over low heat for just a couple minutes, then serve warm over the sautéed tenderloin medallions.

HELPFUL HINT

For a change, try grilling the tenderloins, or even chicken breast, along with portobello mushroom caps. Then use the same blue cheese sauce!

Meat Lasagna

Yes, I've lost my noodles—at least in this lasagna! But I guarantee you won't miss them in this otherwise authentic Italian lasagna. With the wonderfully rich and satisfying ricotta and mozzarella filling, and the spicy Italian seasonings and meat, you'll see it's no big deal to lose your noodles!

YIELD:
8 servings

NET CARBOHYDRATES:
3 grams per serving

PREP:
30 minutes

COOK:
45 to 50 minutes

2 tablespoons olive oil
2 cups diced celery
½ cup diced red onion
2 pounds ground beef
15 ounces sugar-free tomato sauce
1 teaspoon minced fresh garlic
1 teaspoon garlic powder
½ teaspoon salt
½ teaspoon freshly ground black pepper

CHEESE FILLING:
15 ounces ricotta cheese
16 ounces mozzarella cheese, shredded
½ cup grated Parmesan cheese
1 large egg
½ teaspoon minced fresh garlic
2 teaspoons dried Italian seasoning
1 teaspoon garlic powder
¼ teaspoon freshly ground black pepper

Special equipment: 13 x 9-inch baking dish

1. Preheat the oven to 350° F.

2. Heat the oil in a large skillet over medium-high heat. Add the celery and onion and cook until slightly tender.

3. Add the ground beef and cook until browned. Drain off the excess fat with a spoon or turkey baster.

4. Add the tomato sauce, garlic, garlic powder, salt, and pepper and simmer for 2 more minutes, stirring constantly. Remove from the heat.

5. Mix the ingredients for the cheese filling together in a bowl using half the mozzarella.

6. Fill the bottom of the baking dish with the meat filling and top with the cheese filling.

7. Cover the top with the remaining 8 ounces of mozzarella.

8. Bake for 45 to 50 minutes, until the top starts to become golden and bubbly.

9. Let cool for 10 minutes before slicing (the lasagna will hold together better).

HELPFUL HINT

Rachel puts our leftover lasagna into individual microwave containers and freezes them. Then it's easy to thaw only what you want!

Mock Fettuccine Carbonara

This recipe is a great fresh-food alternative to pasta. Spaghetti squash has a neutral flavor and all the texture and visual appeal of real spaghetti. When you add a flavorful topping or a rich sauce, you'll never miss the real thing!

YIELD:
4 servings

NET CARBOHYDRATES:
8 grams per serving

PREP:
20 minutes

COOK:
30 minutes

1 medium spaghetti squash*

CARBONARA SAUCE:
4 tablespoons unsalted butter
½ cup diced Parma ham (you may also use prosciutto, baked ham, or cooked bacon)
½ cup small broccoli florets, lightly blanched
1 cup heavy cream
1 large egg yolk (save the white for your next omelet)
1 clove garlic, crushed
1½ cups freshly grated Parmesan
¼ cup chopped fresh parsley

Salt and freshly ground black pepper
Fresh basil leaves, for garnish
Grape tomatoes, halved, for garnish

1. Cut the squash lengthwise in half. Scoop out the seeds of one half with a spoon. Refrigerate the other half for another meal.

2. Fill a large pot with water and bring to a full boil. Completely submerge the squash half in the boiling water and cook for about 20 to 25 minutes, until you can pierce the inside easily with a fork and the pulp pulls apart in strands.

3. Remove, drain, and plunge the squash half in a pot of cold water or an ice bath to stop the cooking. When the squash is cool, drain and dry it, then use a fork to scrape the cooked squash out of its skin, fluffing and separating the pulp into spaghetti-like strands. Discard the skin.

4. Fill a medium pot with water and bring to a boil. While waiting for the water to boil, prepare the carbonara sauce: Melt 2 tablespoons of the butter in a medium saucepan over medium high-heat. Add the ham and sauté for about 1 minute. Whisk in the cream and egg yolk and cook for 1 to 2 minutes more. Add the garlic and cheese and whisk quickly just to heat through. Remove from the heat and stir in the rest of the butter and the parsley.

5. Right before serving, place the squash strands in a strainer and dip briefly into the pot of boiling water to reheat. Remove and shake off any excess water.

6. Put the hot spaghetti squash on a serving platter. Toss with the carbonara sauce or pour the sauce over the top. Season to taste with salt and pepper. Garnish with fresh basil leaves and grape tomatoes before serving.

*COOK'S TIP: This recipe uses only half the spaghetti squash. Cook and top the other half with butter, sour cream, cheese, and bacon for a mock stuffed baked potato.

Baked Ham with Maple Bourbon Glaze

Family dinners are a very important part of eating *Stella Style*, and they don't get much easier than our recreation of this traditional family favorite. With this recipe, you get all the flavors of the baked ham you've come to love, but without all the sugars found in traditional glazes.

YIELD:
12 servings

NET CARBOHYDRATES:
4 grams per serving

PREP:
15 minutes

COOK:
1½ hours

One 8- to 10-pound hickory-smoked ham (fully cooked), butt portion

GLAZE:
1 teaspoon sugar-free maple extract
1 teaspoon dry mustard
1 teaspoon white vinegar
1¼ cups sugar substitute (Splenda recommended)
2 to 3 tablespoons bourbon

1 tablespoon whole cloves

1. Move the oven rack to the lowest position and preheat the oven to 325° F.

2. Place the ham fatty side up in a shallow baking pan, cover loosely with aluminum foil, and bake for 1 hour to heat it all the way through.

3. While the ham is baking, mix together all the glaze ingredients in a bowl.

4. Remove the heated ham from the oven, take off the foil, and use a sharp knife to make shallow cuts in a tic-tac-toe fashion (making 1-inch squares) all over the fatty side of the ham. Insert a single whole clove into every corner of the squares.

5. Pour the glaze over the top of the ham and let it drip down the sides.

6. Bake the uncovered ham for another 30 minutes.

7. Remove the ham from the oven and let stand for 15 minutes before slicing and serving.

HELPFUL HINTS

We take the leftovers, trim off the fat, and slice it all up for lunchmeats and salads. And try serving Key Lime Cheesecake (page 218) for a delicious low-carb dessert!

Grilled Country-Style Pork Ribs with Bourbon Barbecue Sauce

Country-style pork ribs look just like beef short ribs. They're very meaty and usually inexpensive. What's more, they taste just as good as their more expensive counterpart, back ribs. And you get more meat! This slow-cooking method infuses the barbecue flavor into the pork, gets rid of the fat, and tenderizes the meat until it falls apart! And the sauce, well, don't get me started. You got some cookin' to do! You'll want to finish these on the grill to get that extra flavor and crispness.

YIELD:
6 servings

NET CARBOHYDRATES:
3 grams per serving

PREP:
20 minutes

COOK:
2¾ hours

4 to 5 pounds country-style pork ribs
Salt and freshly ground black pepper
1½ cups No-Cook Bourbon Barbecue Sauce (page 89)
2 cups water

Special equipment: Grill

1. Place the rack in the center of the oven and preheat the oven to 290° F.

2. Season the ribs liberally with salt and pepper on both sides and place in a deep roasting pan just big enough to fit the ribs in a single layer.

3. Pour 1 cup barbecue sauce and 2 cups water over the ribs until they're almost completely submerged. If they're not, add a bit more sauce and water or use a smaller pan.

4. Cover tightly with aluminum foil and bake for about 2½ hours, until the meat is almost falling off the bone.

5. Remove, drain the ribs immediately, and coat with the remaining ½ cup barbecue sauce.

6. Preheat the grill to high. Grill the ribs for just a few minutes on each side before serving.

HELPFUL HINTS

If you have extra sauce, freeze it. Refrigerate the precooked ribs if you don't plan to grill them immediately, then just bring them back to room temperature before grilling.

Anthony's Pork Chops Parmesan

Rachel made this great baked pork chop recipe long before we started low-carb but without the cheese. My older son, Anthony, loves anything "Parmesan" style—that is, with cheese on top—and suggested adding the Parmesan to the breading mix. With one simple substitution (seasoned soy flour in place of bread crumbs) and one small addition (Parmesan cheese) we now enjoy yet one more variation on a classic recipe—*Stella Style!*

YIELD:
4 servings

NET CARBOHYDRATES:
4 grams per serving

PREP:
15 minutes

COOK:
45 minutes

Vegetable oil cooking spray
3 large eggs
¹/₄ cup heavy cream or water

ITALIAN PARMESAN BREADING:
2¹/₃ cups soy flour
2 teaspoons salt
1 teaspoon freshly ground black pepper
1 teaspoon garlic powder
2 tablespoons dried Italian seasoning
1 tablespoon grated Parmesan cheese

8 center-cut bone-in pork chops, about 3 pounds
Salt and freshly ground black pepper to taste

1. Preheat the oven to 375° F. Spray a baking sheet with cooking spray and set aside.

2. In a medium bowl, mix together the eggs and cream to make an egg wash.

3. In a larger bowl, mix together all the breading ingredients.

4. Season the pork chops well with salt and pepper. Dip each first in the breading, then in the egg wash, then back in the breading, making sure to coat well on both sides.

5. Pat off any excess breading and place the chops on the greased baking sheet. Bake for approximately 45 minutes, until the chops are tender and well browned.

Roasted Rosemary Pork Loin

I've been making this naturally low-carb classic since the late '70s when continental French cuisine was becoming more and more popular. Twenty-five years later I'm still making it, and now for dinner parties I stand right there and slice it! It's a great way to entertain and interact with your guests, and it can be served hot or cold!

Vegetable oil cooking spray
One 4-pound boneless pork loin
2 tablespoons Dijon mustard
1 clove garlic, minced
2 tablespoons chopped red onion
2 teaspoons salt
½ teaspoon freshly ground black pepper
2 tablespoons chopped fresh rosemary leaves

YIELD:
12 servings

NET CARBOHYDRATES:
0 grams per serving

PREP:
15 minutes

COOK:
1 hour 20 minutes

1. Preheat the oven to 350° F. Spray a shallow roasting pan with cooking spray and set aside.

2. Trim any excess fat from the pork loin, leaving a wide, thin strip of fat running down the center of the top.

3. Rub the entire pork loin evenly with the mustard, followed by the garlic, red onion, salt, and pepper. Make sure to really rub in the spices.

4. Sprinkle the rosemary evenly over the top.

5. Place the pork loin in the roasting pan and bake for 20 minutes. Reduce the heat to 300° F and continue baking for about 1 hour, until a meat thermometer stuck into the thickest part of the loin registers 145° F.

6. Remove the pork from the oven and let it rest for at least 10 minutes before slicing into 12 medallions.

Tequila-Marinated Grilled Boneless Pork Loin

Seems we can always find whole boneless pork loin for a good price at the market. The trick is to buy the piece whole and cut it yourself. This way you can really reduce the price per pound. After bringing it home, we simply divide it up and freeze what we won't cook in the next few days. We use it to make everything from stir-fry, to roasts, to these grilled loin chops. This is a great one for anytime grilling and just one more way to sneak tequila into a recipe!

YIELD:
8 servings

NET CARBOHYDRATES:
2 grams per serving

PREP:
10 minutes

MARINATE:
4 hours minimum

COOK:
10 minutes

1 fresh jalapeño pepper, seeded
1 clove garlic, peeled
1 cup tequila
1 cup teriyaki sauce
¼ cup sesame oil, optional (omit if you don't like the flavor)
¼ cup Worcestershire sauce
¼ teaspoon kosher salt
¼ teaspoon freshly ground black pepper
1 3-pound boneless pork loin, trimmed and cut into eight 1-inch-thick chops
Fresh cilantro leaves, for garnish

Special equipment: Grill

1. In a food processor or blender, combine all ingredients except the pork loin and cilantro leaves. Process until smooth.

2. Place the loin chops in a nonreactive container, pour the marinade over the top, and turn them to coat both sides. Refrigerate for at least 4 hours before cooking.

3. Preheat the grill to high.

4. Place the marinated chops on the white-hot grill and cook for 4 to 5 minutes on each side (cooking time will vary with the thickness of the chops). Serve garnished with fresh cilantro.

HELPFUL HINT

To make this dish even more flavorful, place a small pat of butter on each cooked pork chop just as it's hot off the grill and serve right as the butter's melting! Mmmm.

Poultry

Poultry, just like fish and seafood, is a great source of lean protein. And while there may not be quite as many varieties of poultry as there are of seafood, don't cry "fowl!"

In this category you'll find everything from basics such as **Chicken with Bacon, Tomato, and Thyme** to **Chili Turkey Burgers**! Here, just like every other *Stella Style* recipe, the key is using your imagination (and putting the leftovers to good use in the days that follow). Chicken and turkey are also the least expensive of the protein group; so, if you have the space, buy whole birds and chicken breasts when they're on sale, then freeze them for later use.

Although we still buy plenty of deli turkey for roll-ups, there's nothing like having a **Traditional Oven-Roasted Turkey** on a platter in the fridge. Whenever you're in the mood, slice a piece off, grab a jar of mayonnaise, and, along with a little cheese, you've got yourself a great snack. And don't throw the carcass out—at least not before you've used it to make a hearty, nutritious soup (try our hearty **Turkey Vegetable Soup** on page 172)!

Tequila Chicken

Chicken with Bacon, Tomato, and Thyme

Southern Fried Chicken

Chili Turkey Burgers

Traditional Oven-Roasted Turkey

Turkey Stroganoff

Tequila Chicken

This is the first recipe Rachel and I ever made on television. We picked it because it's sooo good, it's classic **Stella Style**, and it's simple enough for anyone to make. Definitely a keeper!

YIELD:
4 servings:

NET CARBOHYDRATES:
2 grams per serving

PREP:
10 minutes

COOK:
20 minutes

Vegetable oil cooking spray
2 tablespoons extra-virgin olive oil
1 pound boneless, skinless chicken breast, butterfly cut into
    4 separate fillets
2 tablespoons tequila
2 tablespoons chopped red onion
2 tablespoons chopped fresh cilantro
¼ teaspoon minced fresh garlic
1½ tablespoons ground cumin
½ teaspoon kosher salt
¼ teaspoon freshly ground black pepper
⅛ teaspoon cayenne pepper (2 dashes)
4 ounces Colby Jack cheese, shredded (you may also use
    Cheddar, Monterey Jack, or another similar cheese)
4 tablespoons sour cream
4 tablespoons salsa picante (you can use either my recipe for
    Pico de Gallo on page 91, or store-bought as long as it
    has no added sugars)

1. Preheat the oven to 400° F. Spray a baking sheet with cooking spray and set aside.

2. Place the olive oil, the chicken breast fillets, and all other ingredients except the cheese, sour cream, and salsa into a bowl. Toss until coated.

3. Place the coated filets on the baking sheet and bake for 25 to 30 minutes, until a meat thermometer inserted into the thickest piece of chicken registers at least 165° F.

4. Remove the cooked chicken from the oven, top with the shredded cheese, and return to the oven just long enough for the cheese to melt, about 2 minutes.

5. Serve each piece topped with 1 tablespoon each of sour cream and salsa.

HELPFUL HINT

Use the leftovers to make a great Mexican salad the next day! Just slice up the chicken, serve over romaine lettuce, and top with Guacamole (page 63).

Chicken with Bacon, Tomato, and Thyme

Whenever boneless, skinless chicken breast goes on sale—and that happens pretty often—Rachel buys a shipload and freezes what we're not going to use immediately. That means I have to keep coming with up new, quick recipes for chicken breast. This recipe is the brainchild of one such occasion—right after Rachel's ship came in!

YIELD:
4 servings

NET CARBOHYDRATES:
1 gram per serving

PREP:
15 minutes

COOK:
40 minutes

8 slices bacon (you may also use precooked bacon)
1½ pounds boneless, skinless chicken breast, cut into
    4 pieces
2 tablespoons extra-virgin olive oil
1 clove garlic, minced
Salt and freshly ground black pepper
2 Roma tomatoes
2 tablespoons chopped red onion
1 bunch fresh thyme

1. Preheat the oven to 400° F.

2. If you're not using precooked bacon, half-cook the bacon by laying the slices on a baking sheet and baking for about 10 minutes. Remove, drain on paper towels, and set aside.

3. Working on a baking sheet, coat each chicken breast with olive oil and minced garlic, then sprinkle lightly with salt and pepper.

4. Wrap 2 slices of the bacon crisscross around each piece of chicken, forming an X at the center of each breast.

5. Cut the ends of each Roma tomato and discard (or eat them like I do!). Then cut each tomato into 2 thick slices.

6. Sprinkle each breast with onion, then place a thick slice of tomato on top of the bacon "cross." Tuck a few sprigs of fresh thyme right under the bacon. (You really can't overdo it with the thyme, because you'll remove it before serving.)

7. Arrange the chicken breasts on the baking sheet so that they don't touch one another. Bake about 30 minutes, until the chicken is completely cooked (when it reaches an internal temperature of at least 165° F). Remove the thyme sprigs and discard before serving.

HELPFUL HINTS

This is a great meal to make ahead and freeze for anytime! Try different herbs in place of the thyme for variety. I like dill, basil, or cilantro.

Southern Fried Chicken

When I was growing up in the South, fried chicken was not only a comfort food but also a staple in our diet. With this recipe, I never feel far from home! Eating *Stella Style* doesn't mean you can't have fried foods—you simply replace the traditional flour breading with seasoned soy flour! Rachel and I love to pack a cooler with cold fried chicken and our Waldorf Cole Slaw (page 195) and have a picnic on the shore!

YIELD:
4 servings

NET CARBOHYDRATES:
8 grams per serving

PREP:
20 minutes

COOK:
about 30 minutes

3 to 6 cups vegetable oil (more or less depending on the pot used)
3 large eggs
¼ cup heavy cream or water

BREADING:
2⅓ cups soy flour
2 teaspoons salt
1 teaspoon freshly ground black pepper
1 teaspoon garlic powder
1 teaspoon poultry seasoning

1 whole chicken, cut into 8 pieces, or 3 pounds boneless chicken breast
Salt and freshly ground black pepper

1. Preheat the oven to 350° F.

2. Place a deep, heavy pot over medium-high heat and fill with at least 1 inch vegetable oil for boneless chicken, or at least 2 inches for whole pieces. Heat the oil to 350° F. It's very important to monitor and maintain the temperature, or the soy flour breading, as well as your oil, will burn. (Portable deep fryers are great for this recipe, but if you don't have one, you can use a candy thermometer. Be careful!)

3. In a medium bowl, mix the eggs and cream to make an egg wash.

4. In a larger bowl, mix all the breading ingredients together.

5. Season the chicken well with salt and pepper.

6. Dip each piece first in the breading, then in the egg wash, then back in the breading again, making sure to coat well on all sides. Shake off any excess breading.

7. Carefully place the chicken pieces in the hot oil using a slotted spatula or spoon (wear mitts, please!) and fry until golden brown and crisp—usually just a few minutes is enough.

8. Remove the chicken pieces and drain on paper towels.

9. Place the chicken pieces on a baking sheet. Boneless chicken breasts, if thinly cut, may cook all the way with frying alone, but a cut-up whole chicken will not. Because the soy flour browns long before the chicken is cooked, it's best to finish the chicken by baking in the oven. Bake boneless chicken for 10 minutes, or chicken on the bone for 20 to 25 minutes. A meat thermometer inserted into the thickest part of the chicken should register at least 165° F.

10. Remove the chicken from the oven and serve immediately for the best crunch.

HELPFUL HINTS

Never stray from the fryer when your chicken is in it. Some brands of soy flour are made from toasted soybeans that have already been cooked; they may brown faster than plain flour when frying. Try this same breading for onion rings, baked pork chops, okra, mozzarella sticks, mushrooms, onion rings, and eggplant.

Chili Turkey Burgers

Rachel brought these outrageously different burgers to me one afternoon while I was hard at work on this book. Turkey is an especially lean meat, so you really have to add some moisture to it; Rachel's done that here by using veggies. She made a lot of these, like we always do, to be sure we have leftovers—and I couldn't stop eating them for the next two days! Now, five years after we were introduced to eating low-carb, I've all but forgotten that burgers once came with a bun!

YIELD:
10 burgers

NET CARBOHYDRATES:
1 gram per serving

PREP:
15 minutes

COOK:
12 to 15 minutes

Vegetable oil cooking spray
2½ pounds fresh ground turkey
1 cup shredded sharp Cheddar cheese
1 large egg
½ cup finely diced red bell pepper
¼ cup finely diced red onion
1 tablespoon Quick and Easy Ketchup (page 82)
1 tablespoon chili powder
1 teaspoon salt
¼ teaspoon freshly ground black pepper
Pinch of cayenne pepper

BURGER TOPPINGS:
10 lettuce leaves
1 tomato, cut into 10 slices
1 onion, cut into 10 slices
10 pickle slices
Mayonnaise

1. Spray a large sauté pan with cooking spray and set aside.

2. Put all the turkey burger ingredients into a bowl and mix well with your hands. (You may want to wear plastic gloves, since the chili powder may turn your hands red.)

3. Form the meat mixture into 10 patties.

4. Cook the turkey burgers in the sauté pan over medium-high heat for 6 to 7 minutes on each side, until completely cooked through. (Poultry MUST be fully cooked. No medium-rare for these patties!)

5. Serve as a meal with the traditional burger toppings; feel free to substitute your own low-carb favorites too!

HELPFUL HINT

Pan-frying adds flavor, but if you prefer, you may preheat the oven to 375° F, put the burgers on a baking sheet sprayed with vegetable oil cooking spray, and bake for about 20 minutes, until fully cooked. A meat thermometer inserted into the center of the thickest burger should register at least 165° F.

Traditional Oven-Roasted Turkey

Turkey is a great low-carb meal—and not just for the holidays. It's economical and easy to prepare, and we all know a million uses for the leftovers. So why pay high prices for deli turkey (which may have fillers and added sugars) when you can make your own? This simple classic recipe is so easy that it will fit into any day!

YIELD:
12 to 14 servings

NET CARBOHYDRATES:
0 grams per serving

PREP:
15 minutes

COOK:
5½ to 6½ hours

1 16- to 20-pound turkey
½ cup (1 stick) unsalted butter, softened
Kosher salt
Freshly ground black pepper
Bunches of fresh thyme, parsley, and/or chives, for garnish
Ornamental harvest vegetables, for decoration only*

1. Preheat the oven to 325° F.

2. Remove the giblets and neck from the turkey cavity and save to make stock or gravy. Rinse the turkey well inside and out with cold water and pat dry. Fold the wings across the back of the bird so the tips touch and tie them with heavy kitchen string. Tuck the drumsticks under the strip of skin at the tail or tie together with kitchen string.

3. Place the turkey breast side up in a shallow roasting pan. Spread the butter over the whole turkey and season generously with salt and pepper.

4. Roast the turkey uncovered until it starts to turn golden brown. Loosely tent the bird with aluminum foil and finish cooking until a meat thermometer inserted in the thickest part of the thigh registers 185° F, 5½ to 6½ hours total cooking time.

5. When the turkey is done, remove from the oven and let stand for about 20 minutes before carving. Present the turkey on a large platter garnished with bunches of thyme, parsley, and/or chives and ornamental harvest vegetables.

*COOK'S TIP: You can usually find these ornamental vegetables at your local farmers' market. These pretty miniature gourds are just for decoration; don't eat them!

HELPFUL HINT

Save the drippings for gravy (try the delicious Wild Mushroom Turkey Gravy on page 80) or stock, and keep the carcass to boil for soup stock after you've picked it clean.

Turkey Stroganoff

We've been making this variation on the classic long before we started eating low-carb. It just goes to show that living a low-carb lifestyle doesn't mean you have to throw all your old recipes out with the trash. This meal—like almost everything you cook *Stella Style*—can be changed according to your own taste and the availability of ingredients. Sometimes Rachel makes this with ground beef. It all depends on our mood and what's on sale!

YIELD:
8 servings

NET CARBOHYDRATES:
2.5 grams per serving

PREP:
20 minutes

COOK:
20 minutes

2 tablespoons vegetable oil
2 cups chopped celery
$\frac{1}{3}$ cup chopped red onion
2$\frac{1}{2}$ pounds ground turkey
10 ounces cremini (Baby Bella) or white button mushrooms, sliced
$\frac{1}{4}$ teaspoon minced fresh garlic
1 teaspoon dried tarragon
1$\frac{1}{2}$ teaspoons salt
$\frac{1}{4}$ teaspoons freshly ground black pepper
$\frac{1}{4}$ teaspoon garlic powder
1 cup sour cream
2 tablespoons sliced green onion (scallion) tops

1. Heat the oil in a large skillet over medium-high heat. Add the celery and onion and cook until slightly tender.

2. Add the ground turkey and cook until browned. Drain off the excess fat with a spoon or turkey baster.

3. Add the mushrooms, garlic, and seasonings and simmer for 4 to 5 minutes, stirring constantly.

4. Remove from the heat, stir in the sour cream, and serve, garnished with the scallion tops.

HELPFUL HINT

Traditional stroganoff is served with noodles, a low-carb no-no. Serve these instead with our Garlic Mock Mashed Potatoes (page 181).

Fish and Seafood

For those of you who like your proteins lean, you can't do any better than fish and seafood! And the possibilities—well, there's a whole ocean full of them! Most of the recipes you'll find in this category are classic *Stella Style*—quick, easy-to-prepare, and delicious! There's everything from **Grilled Salmon with Tomato Herb Relish** to **Blackened Sea Scallops with Spinach and Black Soy Beans** and from **Key West Crab Cakes with Mustard Sauce** to **Anaheim Shrimp Scampi**!

Fresh food is one of the most important parts of *Stella Style,* and the key to great fish and seafood is *freshness.* It's always best to deal with someone you know when you're buying seafood, but you should also learn how to recognize fresh seafood and shellfish yourself.

And because you can pay an arm and a leg for a few crab legs, keep an eye out for sales on your favorites too. You can always freeze what you don't cook!

Grilled Salmon with
Tomato Herb Relish

Blackened Sea Scallops
with Spinach and Black
Soy Beans

Anaheim Shrimp
Scampi

Shrimp Mock Fried Rice

Key West Crab Cakes
with Mustard Sauce

Cracked Snow Crab
Martinis

Clams Casino

Mussels Kimchee

Grilled Salmon with Tomato Herb Relish

As good as it is smoked, with a smear of cream cheese and a slice of onion, or as a topping for a Caesar salad, I'll take my salmon grilled anytime. Since it's high in omega-3 fatty acids, which are known to reduce "bad" cholesterol, you can't find a healthier source of protein than salmon. At the Stella household, we try to put it on our menu two to three times a week, which isn't difficult, because it's great for breakfast, lunch, or dinner. This recipe makes you wish for summer all year round!

YIELD:
4 servings

NET CARBOHYDRATES:
3 grams per serving

PREP:
15 minutes

COOK:
10 minutes

3 tablespoons olive oil

RELISH:
3 Roma tomatoes, finely diced
2 tablespoons chopped fresh dill
1 tablespoon chopped fresh Italian parsley
2 tablespoons finely chopped red onion
2 tablespoons rice wine vinegar (you may also use white wine)
1 tablespoon fresh lemon juice
½ teaspoon Worcestershire sauce
¼ teaspoon minced fresh garlic

Four 10-ounce salmon fillets, skin removed
Salt and freshly ground black pepper
Dill and parsley sprigs, for garnish
4 lemon slices, for garnish

Special equipment: Grill or grill pan

1. Preheat a grill to high or an indoor cast-iron grill pan over medium-high heat.

2. Combine 1 tablespoon of the olive oil with all the relish ingredients in a bowl and set aside.

3. Rub the salmon fillets with the remaining 2 tablespoons olive oil and season both sides generously with salt and pepper.

4. Place the salmon on the hot grill and cook each side for only about 4 minutes, until the fish is still a bit undercooked in the center.

5. Remove the fish from the grill, arrange on 4 plates, and spoon the tomato herb relish over each piece. Garnished with fresh herb sprigs and lemon slices and serve.

COOK'S TIP: Salmon should be served a bit on the rare side just as a medium or medium-rare steak would be (overcooking will dry it out).

Blackened Sea Scallops with Spinach and Black Soy Beans

I'll eat "blackened" anything. I love the taste, and it's sooo simple to do! I also love coming home and being able to make dinner in just a few minutes with almost no prep and just one pan. Try this recipe, and you'll see just how easy cooking **Stella Style** gourmet can be!

YIELD:
2 servings

NET CARBOHYDRATES:
2 grams per serving

PREP:
5 minutes

COOK:
5 minutes

2 tablespoons vegetable oil
1 pound fresh sea scallops*
Blackening Spice (page 90)
One 12-ounce can black soy beans, drained and rinsed
    (available at health food and specialty stores)
4 cups fresh spinach leaves, cleaned
2 tablespoons unsalted butter
2 tablespoons sour cream, for garnish, optional

1. Heat the oil in a large, heavy sauté pan or iron skillet over high heat until almost smoking.

2. Coat the scallops well on both sides with the blackening spice (the exact amount isn't crucial; just make sure the scallops are coated liberally) and place them gently in the hot pan. Sear on the first side for about 2 minutes, then turn the scallops over individually and sear for another minute.

3. Add the black beans to one side of the pan, so they heat up separately from the scallops. Throw the fresh spinach and butter right on top of everything and cook it all for about 2 minutes more. The spinach will wilt considerably.

4. To serve, take the spinach off the top and place it in the center of a serving plate. Then arrange the scallops and black beans around it. Garnish with a dollop of sour cream if you like.

*COOK'S TIP: Sea scallops are larger cousins to the tiny bay scallops. Bay scallops are too small for this dish.

HELPFUL HINT

Try this recipe using shrimp or salmon. You can mix and match with *Stella Style!*

Anaheim Shrimp Scampi

Wolfgang Puck launched California Cuisine in the '80s, and eager to put my own spin on the trend, I quickly came up with this recipe, which I named "Anaheim" for no reason other than it was the home of Disneyland! After twenty years, it's one of my most requested recipes!

YIELD:
4 servings

NET CARBOHYDRATES:
4 grams per serving

PREP:
20 minutes

COOK:
6 minutes

1 medium spaghetti squash
6 tablespoons Scampi Butter (page 88)
1 pound (16 to 20 count) peeled and deveined raw shrimp, with tails (tiger prawns recommended)
1 tablespoon white wine
2 ounces Asiago cheese, cut into small chunks
1 avocado, diced into large pieces
Fresh arugula leaves, for garnish

1. Prepare the mock fettuccine using the spaghetti squash, following the directions for Mock Fettuccine Carbonara (page 116). (Save the other half of the squash to make Mock Fettuccine Carbonara.)

2. Place 4 tablespoons of the scampi butter in a large sauté pan over high heat and melt.

3. Add the shrimp and cook for about 2 minutes, stirring occasionally.

4. Add the white wine, which will sizzle in the pan, and cook until the shrimp are opaque, about another 2 minutes.

5. Remove the pan from the heat and stir in the remaining 2 tablespoons scampi butter, the Asiago cheese, and avocado. Serve over the hot spaghetti squash, which you can reheat in a strainer with hot water, as indicated in the fettuccine recipe, and garnish with fresh arugula.

HELPFUL HINT

This recipe is great with fresh sea scallops in place of the shrimp or, even better, use ½ pound of each! The cooking times are identical.

Shrimp Mock Fried Rice

We created this recipe so we wouldn't miss out on one of our favorites—Chinese food! Even though we've avoided white rice since we began eating *Stella Style,* that doesn't mean we can't still enjoy this traditional dish. All we did was substitute grated cauliflower for the rice, without losing any of this recipe's classic flavor!

2 cups raw cauliflower
2 tablespoons vegetable oil
2 tablespoons finely diced green bell peppers
4 tablespoons thinly sliced green onions (scallions)
½ cup cooked salad shrimp
¼ teaspoon minced fresh garlic
3 tablespoons soy sauce
3 large eggs, beaten
Salt to taste, if needed

YIELD:
4 servings

NET CARBOHYDRATES:
3 grams each serving

PREP:
15 minutes

COOK:
8 minutes

1. Grate the fresh cauliflower, using the largest holes of a cheese grater. You can also use a food processor fitted with a grating blade.

2. Heat the oil in a large skillet over medium-high heat. Add the pepper and 3 tablespoons of the onions and cook for 1 minute.

3. Add the cauliflower, shrimp, and garlic and cook, stirring constantly, for 4 to 5 minutes, until the cauliflower is tender.

4. Add the soy sauce and stir. Add the eggs to one corner of the pan but don't stir for 1 minute. This allows the eggs to cook for a bit, which will prevent them from completely breaking up and disappearing into the mix.

5. As soon as the eggs are soft-cooked, remove the skillet from the heat and gently fold the eggs into the mixture. Add salt or more soy sauce to taste. Garnish with the remaining 1 tablespoon green onion and serve.

HELPFUL HINT

In place of the cooked shrimp, try adding an equivalent amount of cooked pork or chicken.

Key West Crab Cakes with Mustard Sauce

Growing up in southern Florida, I always loved the spicy island foods. I remember well at age ten going to Key West with my parents and eating at the most famous seafood restaurants. (Some people went to museums; my family went to restaurants.) I had conch salad, conch chowder, and fried conch—and I loved them all! That time in Key West was a huge influence on my journey to become a chef, and it's exactly what gave me the idea to use some of those same ingredients to make these crab cakes a delightfully different treat—*Stella Style!*

YIELD:
18 servings

NET CARBOHYDRATES:
0 grams

PREP:
20 minutes

COOK:
9 minutes

1 pound blue crabmeat (available in a can or plastic tub in your grocery store's seafood department)
1 tablespoon finely diced red bell pepper
1 tablespoon finely diced green bell pepper
1 tablespoon finely chopped fresh parsley leaves
1 tablespoon mayonnaise
2 large eggs
1 tablespoon baking powder
1 tablespoon Worcestershire sauce
1½ teaspoons Maryland-style crab seasoning (Old Bay recommended)
2 tablespoons canola oil
Mustard Sauce (page 83)

1. In a large bowl, mix all ingredients except the oil and sauce.

2. Heat the oil in a large skillet over medium-high heat. Carefully spoon the batter in rounded tablespoons into the pan. (The resulting crab cakes will be the size of poker chips, and the batter will be very loose since this recipe has no bread crumbs. Once the egg in the mixture starts to cook, the crab cakes will hold together fine.)

3. Cook the crab cakes on one side until firm, about 2 minutes, then flip and cook on the other side for about 1 more minute. Continue cooking in batches until you've used up all the batter. Serve hot with Mustard Sauce.

Cracked Snow Crab Martinis

This is an elegant and fun way to present a special appetizer for the holidays or any other memorable occasion. Serving seafood at Christmas and other holidays was a tradition in our Italian-American family, and this was always a favorite of my mother's. I'm sure you'll like it too!

12 fully cooked fresh or frozen snow crab claws* (you may substitute cooked jumbo shrimp, peeled and chilled)
6 ounces mesclun lettuce mix (any delicate salad mix will work)
6 tablespoons Mustard Sauce (page 83)
1 lemon, cut into 6 wedges

Special equipment: 6 martini glasses (coupe champagne glasses are fine, too)
6 cocktail forks

YIELD:
6 servings

NET CARBOHYDRATES:
4 grams per serving

PREP:
10 minutes

1. If they're frozen, thaw the crab claws but keep them chilled on ice.

2. Fill each martini glass halfway with the mesclun lettuce mix.

3. Place 2 cracked crab claws in each glass with the pincers pointing upward and over the edge of the glass. Leave a space in the center of each glass.

4. Put 1 tablespoon of the mustard sauce in the center of each glass.

5. Thread each lemon wedge onto a small cocktail fork and stick into the glass like a swizzle stick for a drink. Serve immediately.

*COOK'S TIP: Snow crab claws typically come frozen and "cracked" and are usually available during the holidays. If you can't find just the crab claws, ask the clerk at your local seafood counter for a few of the claws off the snow crab clusters that they always have on hand. They won't want to break them off the clusters, but there are always loose ones! And if you buy the whole clusters, you can use the crabmeat in the legs to make Key West Crab Cakes with Mustard Sauce (page 146) or Crab-Stuffed Mushrooms (page 68)!

Clams Casino

Coming from an Italian-American family, I looked forward to clams at every holiday meal. Whether they were steamed, baked, fried, or just raw on the half shell, WE ALL LOVED CLAMS! This recipe is our holiday favorite, but it's sooo good and sooo easy to make that it's a shame to limit to it to just the holidays. So whenever the clams look good at the seafood counter, treat yourself to this great, easy-to-prepare, foolproof recipe. After all, any day can be a holiday!

YIELD:
4 servings

NET CARBOHYDRATES:
2 grams per serving

PREP:
20 minutes

COOK:
5 minutes

1 dozen raw cherrystone clams

CASINO BUTTER (makes enough for 3 dozen clams):
½ cup (1 stick) unsalted butter, softened
3 tablespoons minced red onion
1 tablespoon minced fresh garlic
1 tablespoon diced red bell pepper
1 tablespoon diced green bell pepper
1 tablespoon crumbled cooked bacon or bacon bits
1 tablespoon chopped fresh parsley
½ teaspoon garlic powder
½ teaspoon kosher salt
¼ teaspoon freshly ground black pepper
Dash of white pepper
Dash of Worcestershire sauce
Juice of 1 lemon
1 tablespoon white wine

1. Place the rack in the center of the oven and set the oven to broil.

2. Place all the casino butter ingredients in a small bowl and whisk together until combined. (Make sure the butter is soft but not completely melted, or it won't combine easily.)

3. Place the unopened clams on a baking sheet and put them in the hot oven for a minute or two; this will make it easier for you to open them. Take them out of the oven and cool slightly for a few minutes before opening. Return the clams on the half shell to the baking sheet.

4. Top each clam with about 1 teaspoon of the butter. Broil on the center rack for about 5 minutes, until the butter starts to bubble and brown slightly. Remove and serve hot.

HELPFUL HINTS

You can also make this recipe using oysters, vegetables, or fish. Top whatever you're cooking with the casino butter and bake, broil, sauté, or grill! Wrap the leftover butter in plastic wrap and freeze it for your next dish.

Mussels Kimchee

Back in the '80s, I fell in love with Mussels Fra Diavolo. The devilish mixture of mussels and cayenne pepper was a witches' brew—I couldn't resist it. Years later, when I tried my hand at Pacific Rim cuisine, I couldn't help trying to reinvent this personal favorite. The difference is small but important; in this variation the heat comes from the kimchee (hot, spicy pickled Korean cabbage). Best of all, it's all naturally low-carb!

YIELD:
6 servings

NET CARBOHYDRATES:
3 grams per serving

PREP:
15 minutes

COOK:
6 minutes

2 tablespoons olive oil
2 cups diced Roma tomatoes
2 tablespoons chopped red onion
2 tablespoons chopped fresh basil
1 teaspoon minced fresh garlic
1/2 teaspoon salt
2 pounds fresh mussels, washed and debearded*
1/2 cup kimchee (you can find this in a jar or fresh at Asian food markets)
2 ounces red wine (any dry variety will do)
Fresh basil leaves, for garnish

1. Heat the olive oil in a large sauté pan over medium-high heat. Add the tomatoes, onion, basil, garlic, and salt and cook for 1 minute.

2. Add the cleaned mussels to the pan, top with the kimchee, then pour the wine over everything.

3. Cover and cook for 4 to 5 more minutes, until the mussels begin to open. (Discard any mussels that don't open; this means they're not fresh.) Divide among 6 large soup bowls or serve on a platter with the sauce poured over the mussels. Garnish with fresh basil leaves.

*COOK'S TIP: Never buy opened mussels; they're not fresh. To debeard them, grab the exposed "beard" tightly and pull with an upward jerk to remove.

HELPFUL HINT

You can make the sauce richer by stirring in a couple pats of butter after cooking.

Vegetarian Entrées

ome of you may be surprised to see that this book even has a vegetarian entrée category, given low-carb's reputation of being nothing more than meat and eggs. Well, feast your eyes on this list of mouthwatering, low-carb, **vegetarian** recipes! The next time someone tells you that low-carb means meat only, just stick a tasty **Bald Calzone** in front of him. And if that doesn't do the trick, then try my **Three-Cheese Veggie Quesadillas** or my son Christian's **Szechuan Vegetable Stir-Fry**!

Again, despite what many people think, there are many low-carb vegetables to choose from and so many ways to prepare them—*Stella Style,* of course. Just remember to keep a carbohydrate counter handy when you're substituting one vegetable for another of your favorites—that way you can keep everything low-carb.

Szechuan Vegetable
Stir-Fry

Three-Cheese Veggie
Quesadillas

Vegetable Egg Foo
Yung

Vegetable Soufflé

Bald Calzone

Szechuan Vegetable Stir-Fry

We're all Chinese food lovers, especially my youngest son, Christian. Stir-fry is not only one of his favorite meals to eat, it's also one of his favorites to make. (He's into both low-carb and low-fat, so it's really perfect for him.) I love spicy food, so I add the kimchee—a really hot Korean pickled cabbage. Now go get some chopsticks and have some fun!

YIELD:
8 servings

NET CARBOHYDRATES:
8 grams per serving

PREP:
40 minutes

COOK:
5 minutes

3 tablespoons canola oil
1 red bell pepper, julienned
1 green bell pepper, julienned
1 yellow bell pepper, julienned
½ cup julienned red onion
½ small yellow squash, halved lengthwise and cut into thick half-moon slices (1 cup)
½ small zucchini, halved lengthwise and cut into thick half-moon slices (1 cup)
1 baby eggplant, cut into 1-inch squares (1 cup)
1 clove garlic, minced
1 to 2 tablespoons minced fresh ginger
4 tablespoons sesame oil
½ cup teriyaki sauce (average 2 grams sugar per serving)
½ cup canned straw mushrooms
3 cups sliced bok choy
2 cups fresh bean sprouts
⅓ cup sliced bamboo shoots
1 teaspoon garlic powder
½ teaspoon freshly ground black pepper
½ teaspoon kosher salt
⅛ teaspoon cayenne pepper, optional
½ cup snow peas
½ cup kimchee, for garnish, optional

1. Start by preparing and cutting all the vegetables and measuring all the ingredients so that they are ready to go. Once you begin stir-frying, it goes very quickly.

2. In a wok or large sauté pan, heat the oil over high heat to almost smoking. Stirring constantly, add the peppers and onion one type at a time, then follow with the squash, zucchini, eggplant, garlic, ginger, sesame oil, and teriyaki sauce.

3. Cook for about 2 minutes, then add the remaining ingredients and seasonings except for the snow peas and kimchee. Cook about 2 minutes more.

4. Stir in the snow peas and remove from the heat. Serve immediately. Garnish with kimchee if you like it hot!

HELPFUL HINT

Try adding chicken, beef, or pork strips to make other great meals in this style. Use your one additional ingredient or a combination of two or three! And don't forget the shrimp and scallops!

Three-Cheese Veggie Quesadillas

Quesadillas were always a favorite of Christian's, and once we switched to low-carb, I switched to our soy flour pizza crust to keep them on the menu. And the fillings? Well, they're all naturally low-carb anyway. Making these takes more time than just sticking something in the microwave, but the wait is worth it! If you have the time, let the kids join in. They'll love making these—and eating them too!

YIELD:
4 servings

NET CARBOHYDRATES:
8 grams per serving

PREP:
30 minutes

COOK:
10 minutes

3 tablespoons canola oil
1 medium yellow squash, cut into thin circles
1 red bell pepper, julienned
1 green bell pepper, julienned
1 small red onion, thinly sliced
1 clove garlic, minced
¼ teaspoon kosher salt
⅛ teaspoon freshly ground black pepper
2 dashes cayenne pepper
1 teaspoon ground cumin
1 tablespoon tequila, optional
4 ounces Colby cheese, shredded
4 ounces Monterey Jack, shredded
4 ounces Cheddar cheese, shredded
Dough for 1 pizza crust, cooked (page 58)*
2 tablespoons unsalted butter
2 tablespoons finely chopped cilantro leaves
2 tablespoons sliced green onions (scallions)

1. In a large sauté pan or wok, heat the oil over high heat.

2. Add the squash, peppers, onion, garlic, salt, pepper, cayenne, and cumin to the hot oil. Cook for about 1 minute. Remove the pan from the heat and add the tequila (if using). Return the pan to the heat and cook for just a minute or two more and put to the side. If you're not using the tequila, simply cook for a total of 2 to 3 minutes.

3. Combine the shredded cheeses and set aside.

4. Cut the cooked pizza crust into 4 triangular pieces. On 2 pieces layer half of the cheese, cooked veggie mixture, the remaining cheese, and then cover with the two remaining pieces of the crust.

5. Melt the butter in a sauté pan over medium-high heat. When the pan is very hot, carefully place one of the quesadillas in the pan and cook for about 2 minutes on each side, until they're golden brown and the cheese is melted. Repeat with the second quesadilla.

6. Cut each quesadilla into 3 pieces. Garnish with cilantro and scallions before serving.

*COOK'S TIP: The pizza crust recipe makes two crusts, but this recipe only uses one. Wrap the leftover crust in plastic wrap and freeze it for another quickie pizza or quesadilla.

HELPFUL HINT

Try adding your own favorite fillings, such as cooked chicken strips or even lobster! Or try serving them with Guacamole (page 63), my Pico de Gallo (page 91), or sour cream.

Vegetable Egg Foo Yung

This basic recipe allows you to use your imagination. There are so many variations that you could make a different one every day for a year. (I happen to be partial to shrimp, but this time we're going with Rachel's favorite!) This Chinese comfort food is naturally low-carb except for the sauce, but that's no longer a problem, because we've reinvented it—*Stella Style!*

YIELD:
4 servings

NET CARBOHYDRATES:
2 grams per serving

PREP:
20 minutes

COOK:
12 minutes

4 tablespoons canola oil
1/4 cup chopped yellow onion
2 cups shredded cabbage
6 large eggs
1 tablespoon soy sauce
1/2 teaspoon minced fresh garlic
1/4 teaspoon salt
1/8 teaspoon freshly ground black pepper
1/4 cup sliced bamboo shoots
2 tablespoons sliced green onion (scallion) tops, for garnish

1. Place 2 tablespoons of the canola oil in a large pan over medium-high heat. Add the onion and cabbage and cook until tender. Remove from the heat and drain the excess liquid.

2. Whisk the eggs in a bowl and mix in the soy sauce, garlic, seasonings, drained cabbage mixture, and bamboo shoots.

3. Heat the remaining 2 tablespoons canola oil in a large, nonstick pan over medium-high heat.

4. Ladle about 1/2 cup of the egg mixture into the hot pan, as you would for pancakes, and cook for about 3 minutes, until the edges start to brown (or until when jiggled, the pancake starts to slide around in the pan).

5. Flip and cook the pancake for another 2 to 3 minutes, until cooked through.

Repeat, making 3 more pancakes from the egg mixture. Arrange on a serving platter and garnish with scallions before serving warm.

HELPFUL HINTS

If the egg foo yung browns too quickly, finish it by baking it in a preheated 350° F oven for a few minutes. Try making this dish with precooked chicken, beef, or pork strips, or with my favorite, shrimp!

Vegetable Soufflé

Vegetables can quickly become boring, but only if they don't get the attention they deserve! We've always been veggie lovers around here, and going low-carb hasn't changed that. Don't let misconceptions and misinformation keep you from sticking to your greens. We actually eat a greater variety of vegetables now than ever before, and this recipe is one great way to keep them exciting. This dish looks almost as good as it tastes! You can serve it as a meal by itself, as an exciting side dish, or as an appetizer—*Stella Style!*

YIELD:
8 servings

NET CARBOHYDRATES:
3 grams per serving

PREP:
20 minutes

COOK:
1 hour

Vegetable oil cooking spray
6 large eggs
¾ cup heavy cream
½ teaspoon salt
⅛ teaspoon freshly ground black pepper
Dash of ground white pepper
Dash of ground nutmeg
½ cup shredded sharp Cheddar cheese or ½ cup any shredded cheese
½ cup shredded Swiss cheese or ½ cup any shredded cheese
⅓ cup zucchini, cut into large pieces
⅓ cup yellow squash, cut into large pieces
¼ cup diced red bell pepper
¼ cup diced green bell pepper
1½ tablespoons finely diced red onion
1½ tablespoons chopped fresh parsley

Special equipment: 5 x 9-inch loaf pan

1. Preheat a water bath in the oven to 400° F. Spray the loaf pan with cooking spray and set aside.

2. In a large bowl, mix the eggs, cream, salt, both peppers, and the nutmeg together, then pour into the prepared loaf pan.

3. Sprinkle both cheeses and the vegetables over the top, dispersing them evenly, then push it all down into the egg mixture with your hands or the back of a spoon.

4. Place loaf pan in water bath and bake for about 1 hour, until the top turns golden brown and toothpick stuck in the center comes out clean. (If top browns too quickly, cover with a piece of waxed paper sprayed with vegetable oil.)

5. Cool for at least 15 minutes, then cut into 8 thick slices. Carefully remove the slices from the pan and cut each one diagonally in half before serving.

HELPFUL HINT

You can reinvent this recipe over and over by replacing the veggies and cheese with your own favorites. For instance, try using broccoli and cauliflower in place of the zucchini and squash.

Bald Calzone

Okay, I admit it. This recipe is just plain cheesy. We already lost our noodles in our Meat Lasagna (page 114)—and here we can't even get sauced! Seriously though, Rachel reinvented this recipe years ago, and now it's become one of our favorites. If you grew up—like the Stellas did—eating calzones, then it's hard to think of going through life without them. Lucky for you, if you're eating *Stella Style,* you don't have to go without!

YIELD:
8 servings

NET CARBOHYDRATES:
3 grams per serving

PREP:
15 minutes

COOK:
30 to 35 minutes

CHEESE FILLING:
Vegetable oil cooking spray
15 ounces whole-milk ricotta cheese
8 ounces mozzarella cheese, shredded
½ cup grated Parmesan cheese
1 large egg
½ teaspoon minced fresh garlic
2 teaspoons dried Italian seasoning
1 teaspoon garlic powder
¼ teaspoon freshly ground black pepper

8 ounces mozzarella cheese, shredded

Special equipment: 8-inch square baking dish

1. Preheat the oven to 350° F. Spray a baking dish with cooking spray and set aside.

2. Mix the cheese filling ingredients together in a bowl and spread in the baking dish.

3. Cover the top with the remaining 8 ounces shredded mozzarella cheese.

4. Bake for 35 to 40 minutes, until the top starts to become golden and bubbly.

5. Let cool for 10 minutes before slicing, so the calzone will hold together better.

HELPFUL HINT

Serve with the pizza sauce from our Low-Carb Pizza (page 58) as a great complement!

Salads and Soups

Salads and soups are perfect for low-carbing *Stella Style!* A bowl of lettuce is only a couple carbs, and most salad toppings (like chicken, meat, fish, cheese, and vegetables) are low in carbohydrates too. Naturally, we've reinvented the classics—such as **Caesar Salad** and **Cole Slaw**—so you won't miss your old favorites. And if you'd rather just have a simple, mixed green salad, then turn to the Thousand Island Dressing and Greek Dressing recipes (pages 93 and 94)—reinvented *Stella Style,* of course!

Our soups, too, are naturally low-carb meals. They're also easy to cook in big batches, and easy to store—either in the refrigerator or the freezer—for a quick anytime meal. In this section, my mom gets into the act again with **Mamma Stella's Stracciatella,** and we mix seafood and soup together for our **Seafood Cioppino.** And don't forget to reinvent your old standbys. I snuck cauliflower in and potatoes out for our delicious **Ham and Mock Potato Soup** and came up with another low-carb classic—*Stella Style!*

Key West Caesar Salad

George's Gorgonzola Salad

Ginger Salad

Ernie's Greek Salad

Minute Steak Salad

Cucumber and Tomato Salad

Radicchio Salad with Quick Raspberry Vinaigrette

Ginny's Taco Salad

Turkey Vegetable Soup

Mamma Stella's Straciatella Soup

Ham and Mock Potato Soup

Seafood Cioppino

Key West Caesar Salad

For those of you just starting a low-carb lifestyle, salad plays an important part in changing the way you eat. It's a virtually zero-carb food, and romaine lettuce is a great source of fiber. Plus you can make a whole meal out of a bowl of it simply by topping it with beef, chicken, fish, or eggs. The Key lime twist I put on the traditional version is just one more result of my love for Key West!

YIELD:
4 servings

NET CARBOHYDRATES:
1 gram per serving

PREP:
15 minutes

DRESSING:
2 large egg yolks (save the whites for an omelet)
1 teaspoon Dijon mustard
1 small clove garlic, peeled
1/8 teaspoon freshly ground black pepper
1 teaspoon Worcestershire sauce
1/2 teaspoon anchovy paste
1/4 cup extra-virgin olive oil
1/2 cup canola oil
3 tablespoons Key lime juice (the juice from 2 fresh limes; if Key limes are not available, substitute regular limes or bottled lime juice)
1/4 cup finely grated Parmesan cheese
Kosher salt

1 head romaine lettuce
2 tablespoons diced red bell pepper
2 tablespoons diced yellow bell pepper
2 tablespoons chopped fresh parsley
2 tablespoons finely grated Parmesan cheese
1/2 lime, cut into 4 slices, for garnish

1. Make the dressing: In a food processor or blender, combine the egg yolks, mustard, garlic, pepper, Worcestershire sauce, and anchovy paste. Process on medium until completely blended. With the food processor or blender on low, slowly pour in the olive oil in a continuous, steady steam, then add the canola oil and lime juice the same way. Pour the dressing into a small bowl or glass container and add the Parmesan cheese. Add salt to taste.

2. Rinse the romaine well with very cold water and pat dry. Tear off the tough outer green part of the leaves and the tough white stems and discard. Tear the leaves into bite-sized pieces.

3. Toss the torn romaine with the Caesar dressing, then divide among 4 bowls. Sprinkle the bell peppers on top and chopped parsley around the edges of each bowl. Sprinkle with the grated Parmesan cheese and garnish with the lime slices.

George's Gorgonzola Salad

Blue cheese dressing is almost always zero carb, so pour it on to your heart's content! It's been a personal favorite of mine long before I switched to low-carb, so you can imagine how happy I was when I found out I could still eat as much as I wanted. I chose the ingredients in this hearty salad to perfectly complement the Gorgonzola blue cheese. This salad can be paired with many entrées—or it can make a great stand-alone meal!

YIELD:
4 servings

NET CARBOHYDRATES:
1.5 grams per serving
(with 1 ounce dressing)

PREP:
10 minutes

1 cup fresh green beans
½ cup mayonnaise
½ teaspoon Worcestershire sauce
6 ounces Gorgonzola cheese
Salt and freshly ground black pepper to taste
1 head radicchio lettuce, rinsed and cored, leaves left whole
1 head romaine lettuce, rinsed and torn into bite-sized pieces (may be bought in a bag)
½ cup grape tomatoes, halved (you may use cherry tomatoes or omit them altogether for a lower-carb meal)
⅓ cup walnut halves

1. Bring a small pot of water to a boil. Cut the ends off the green beans, drop them into the boiling water, and cook for 5 to 7 minutes, until tender.

2. Drain the beans and cool them in an ice bath or under running cold water to stop the cooking. Drain the beans again, cut them in half, and reserve.

3. In a bowl, mix the mayonnaise and Worcestershire sauce. Gently fold in two thirds of the blue cheese (4 ounces), saving the rest for topping the salad. Season the dressing with salt and pepper to taste.

4. Line 4 bowls or plates with the whole radicchio leaves and pile the romaine lettuce high in the center.

5. Spoon Gorgonzola dressing over each salad, then top with a few green beans, crumbled Gorgonzola, grape tomatoes, and walnut halves before serving.

HELPFUL HINT

Make this salad into a complete meal by topping it with chicken breast, steak, or salmon!

Ginger Salad

Salad is great for eating *Stella Style,* with only about one carb for a whole bowl of any lettuce, and this is a refreshingly different way to enjoy salad. I originally invented this dish for a cooking class on Pacific Rim cuisine, and since then it has become a regular around our house. The rice wine vinegar and ginger make a great combination of flavors!

YIELD:
4 servings

NET CARBOHYDRATES:
1 gram per serving

PREP:
10 minutes

1 tablespoon Dijon mustard
1 tablespoon fresh lemon juice
2 tablespoons rice wine vinegar
1 tablespoon minced fresh ginger
¾ cup canola oil
Kosher salt to taste
⅛ teaspoon freshly ground black pepper
½ head iceberg lettuce, shredded (or use your preferred lettuce)
2 tablespoons chopped fresh parsley leaves
Lemon slices, for garnish

1. In a blender or food processor on high speed, combine the mustard, lemon juice, vinegar, and ginger for just a few seconds until smooth. Turn the blender to a lower speed and slowly add the oil in a continuous stream.

2. Season with salt and pepper to taste.

3. Pile the shredded lettuce high in the center of a large bowl. Pour the dressing over the lettuce and toss. Sprinkle the fresh parsley around the edges of the bowl and garnish with lemon slices.

HELPFUL HINT

You can use dinner leftovers, such as chicken breast, salmon, and shrimp, to top this salad.

Ernie's Greek Salad

Ernie is Rachel's father, and although Greek Salad is actually Rachel's favorite, he loves it too. (We've put recipes from almost all of our family members into this book, and we didn't want to ignore my father-in-law.) Rachel's dad is a great cook and actually does much of the holiday cooking when we visit. He's best known for the Maple Syrup Eggs he's made for the whole family every Easter morning since Rachel was a kid! (We'll try tackling that one in the next book!)

4 cups mixed salad greens (your choice)
½ cup sliced cucumber (keep the skin on so you keep the vitamins in!)
¼ cup thinly sliced red onion
4 ounces feta cheese, coarsely crumbled
1 Roma tomato, quartered
4 pieces pepperoncini peppers (or more, if you like!)
2 ounces Kalamata olives (you may use any Greek or Italian marinated olives)

YIELD:
2 servings

NET CARBOHYDRATES:
3 grams per serving

PREP:
15 minutes

1. Divide the lettuce between 2 bowls and pile it high.

2. Top each with cucumber, onion, and feta.

3. Place 2 tomato wedges, 2 pepperoncinis, and a few olives on each of the salads.

HELPFUL HINT

Of course, this salad is best with our Greek Dressing (page 94) or just plain oil and vinegar.

Minute Steak Salad

This was Anthony and Christian's favorite when we first started eating *Stella Style*—and by that, I mean their favorite to eat, and their favorite to make. This recipe is especially easy for anyone just starting to get comfortable in the kitchen. And just like bacon and eggs, it's perfect for either breakfast or lunch.

YIELD:
2 servings

NET CARBOHYDRATES:
4 grams per serving

PREP:
8 minutes

COOK:
8 minutes

2 tablespoons unsalted butter or canola oil
1 cup fresh or frozen sliced red and green bell peppers
12 ounces leftover cooked steak, shredded (thawed frozen minute steaks are great too!)
¼ teaspoon garlic powder
Salt and freshly ground black pepper to taste
1 cup shredded mozzarella cheese (or any cheese you like)
10 ounces mixed salad greens (you can use a prepared mix or a combination of shredded iceberg and romaine)

1. Heat the butter or oil in a large skillet over medium-high heat. Add the peppers, steak, and seasonings and cook for about 5 minutes, until the peppers are tender.

2. Turn the heat off. Top the hot steak and peppers with the cheese and let melt.

3. Divide the salad greens evenly between 2 bowls.

4. Divide the hot mixture evenly between the bowls of salad and serve immediately.

HELPFUL HINT

When you order a steak sandwich at your local sandwich shop, ask them to substitute a salad for the bread. I've never found one that wasn't happy to make the change!

Cucumber and Tomato Salad

This is a cool summer salad that anyone can whip up in a jiffy! My mother used to make this when I was growing up, and all I had to do to keep it on the menu was to replace the sugar with sugar substitute. It still tastes great, just like I remember it, with just a hint of sweetness that's bound to make it one of your family's favorites!

1 cup red wine vinegar
2 tablespoons sugar substitute (Splenda recommended)
1 tablespoon chopped fresh Italian parsley
½ teaspoon salt
2 seedless cucumbers, peeled and thinly sliced
3 Roma tomatoes, cut into wedges
½ red onion, thinly sliced

YIELD:
8 servings

NET CARBOHYDRATES:
2 grams per serving

PREP:
15 minutes

CHILL:
1 hour

1. In a large bowl, combine the vinegar, sugar substitute, parsley, and salt.

2. Add the cucumbers, tomatoes, and onion and toss well. Cover and refrigerate for at least 1 hour before serving chilled.

Radicchio Salad with Quick Raspberry Vinaigrette

These days fresh raspberries always seem to be available at the market. Whenever I see them, I just can't help tasting them—and then I just have to buy some. As a result, we've come up with a bunch of fresh raspberry recipes! This is one that takes only a few minutes, yet tastes like it's from a five-star restaurant!

YIELD:
4 servings

NET CARBOHYDRATES:
7 grams per serving

PREP:
10 minutes

16 ounces sugar-free Italian dressing
1 cup fresh raspberries
¼ cup sugar substitute (Splenda recommended)
1 head radicchio lettuce, leaves separated, rinsed, and dried
One 8-ounce bag fancy lettuce mix (with herbs)
2 Roma tomatoes, each cut into 4 wedges, optional
8 ounces whole hearts of palm, cut into sticks
1 tablespoon minced red bell pepper
1 tablespoon minced green bell pepper

1. In a blender or food processor, combine the Italian dressing, ½ cup of the raspberries, and the sugar substitute. Blend until smooth.

2. Line a bowl or plate with whole radicchio leaves, then pile the fancy lettuce mix high in the center. Place the tomato wedges if using around the plate in a starburst fashion. Add the heart of palm sticks between the wedges.

3. Sprinkle with the minced bell peppers.

4. Pour raspberry vinaigrette over the salad, top with the remaining ½ cup fresh raspberries, and serve. Store the remainder of the vinaigrette (for up to 2 weeks) in the refrigerator.

HELPFUL HINT

Dinner leftovers are great for topping this salad. We like it topped with salmon, chicken, or steak!

Ginny's Taco Salad

This is my sister Virginia's favorite salad, and since I think of her every time we make it, I figured I'd name it after her! We always have chili leftovers in the freezer, and like I've said before, I'll put anything on a salad! I picked iceberg lettuce because it's my favorite, but you can use any lettuce you like. And don't scrimp! A whole bowl of lettuce is only one carb.

4 cups shredded iceberg lettuce
2 cups Black Soy Bean Chili (page 98)
1 cup shredded Colby Jack cheese (you may substitute any
    cheese you prefer)
2 tablespoons chopped red onion
1 Roma tomato, diced
2 tablespoons sour cream
1 tablespoon sliced black olives
1 tablespoon sliced green onion (scallion) tops

> YIELD:
> 2 servings
>
> NET CARBOHYDRATES:
> 4 grams per serving
>
> PREP:
> 15 minutes

1. Divide the shredded lettuce between 2 bowls and pile it high.

2. If the chili isn't hot already, warm it in the microwave.

3. Top each bowl of lettuce with 1 cup chili and ½ cup shredded cheese.

4. Top the salads with the tomato, sour cream, sliced olives, and scallion tops. Serve immediately, while the chili is hot and the salad is cold.

HELPFUL HINT

Rachel loves this taco salad with a scoop of Guacamole (page 63) on top!

Turkey Vegetable Soup

This soup is a great way to get the most out of your holiday leftovers! Don't throw that turkey carcass out—throw it into a pot of water with whatever vegetables you can find in the fridge. And if you don't feel like eating turkey so soon after the holiday, you can wrap and freeze the carcass to pick at later, or you can make the soup and freeze it. It'll stay good for months and is a perfect ready-when-you-are meal!

YIELD:
6 servings

NET CARBOHYDRATES:
2 grams per serving

PREP:
15 minutes

COOK:
3 hours

1 roasted turkey carcass
8 cups water
½ white onion, peeled and quartered
3 ribs celery, cut into large chunks
2 bay leaves
1 teaspoon dried sage
1 teaspoon poultry seasoning
2 tablespoons butter or vegetable oil
1 cup diced onions
2 cups diced celery
2 cups sautéed spinach or another leftover vegetable
2 cups diced cooked turkey (the dark meat from the legs is perfect!)
2 tablespoons minced fresh parsley
Salt and freshly ground black pepper to taste

1. Place the turkey carcass in a large stockpot. Add the water along with the quartered onion, celery chunks, bay leaves, sage, and poultry seasoning and bring to a simmer. (Don't let the soup come to a rapid boil.)

2. Simmer for 2½ hours. Remove from the heat and strain the stock.

3. Add the butter, diced onions and diced celery, to a large pot and cook just until tender.

4. Pour in the turkey stock and bring to a simmer.

5. Stir in the spinach, diced turkey, and parsley. Season to taste with salt and pepper and serve.

HELPFUL HINTS

You can freeze the turkey broth and use it in place of chicken stock in any recipe. (Cats love the meat you get from the carcass after you make the stock—at least mine do! Just keep them away from the bones.)

Mamma Stella's Stracciatella Soup

Try saying that three times in a row! This one I just had to name after my mother, because she made it for me every time I had a cold. Stracciatella is best described as an Italian egg drop soup. It takes only minutes to make and is naturally low-carb. Try it as a starter for my Anaheim Shrimp Scampi (page 144). Ciao down, Bella!

YIELD:
6 servings

NET CARBOHYDRATES:
1 gram per serving

PREP:
5 minutes

COOK:
12 minutes

6 cups chicken stock
3 large eggs
¼ cup grated Parmesan cheese
2 tablespoons chopped fresh parsley
Salt and freshly ground black pepper

1. Bring the stock to a simmer in a medium saucepan.

2. Whisk the eggs and Parmesan cheese together in a bowl.

3. Keeping the stock at a simmer, not a boil, slowly pour in the egg mixture, and wait just a minute for it to set.

4. Gently stir in the parsley, slightly breaking up the cooked egg with a wooden spoon.

5. Turn off the heat and season with salt and pepper to taste.

HELPFUL HINTS

This soup is great made with turkey stock from the Turkey Vegetable Soup (page 172). If you substitute sliced scallions for the Parmesan cheese and the parsley, you have a great Chinese egg drop soup. It goes perfectly with Vegetable Egg Foo Yung, (page 156) and Szechuan Vegetables Stir-Fry (page 152).

Ham and Mock Potato Soup

I think this is as good as any vichyssoise—or classic French potato soup—I've ever tasted. I use cauliflower in place of the potatoes, and the combination of tastes is superb. You can enjoy it as a creamy soup, or you can throw in some leftover veggies for a hearty chowder. Just one more reinvention of a classic—**Stella Style**!

6 cups chicken or turkey stock (pages 172–73)
1 medium head cauliflower, cored and cut into small pieces
2 tablespoons butter
1½ cups finely diced Parma ham (you may use any ham or
    cooked bacon)
½ cup thinly sliced leeks or diced white onion
½ clove garlic, minced
1 cup heavy cream
⅛ teaspoon ground white pepper
Salt and freshly ground black pepper
1 tablespoon chopped fresh chives or tender leek tops, for garnish

YIELD:
4 servings

NET CARBOHYDRATES:
4 grams per serving

PREP:
15 minutes

COOK:
10 minutes

1. Put the stock into a large pot and bring to a boil.

2. Add the cauliflower to the boiling stock and cook for about 6 minutes, until tender.

3. Use an immersion or regular blender to purée the cooked cauliflower with the stock. Keep hot.

4. Heat the butter in a large skillet over medium-high heat. Add the ham, leeks, and garlic and cook until slightly tender.

5. Stir the ham mixture into the puréed stock along with the cream and white pepper. Add salt and pepper to taste.

6. Serve in soup bowls and garnish with the chopped chives.

HELPFUL HINT

This soup is even better topped with shredded Cheddar cheese and a dollop of sour cream!

Seafood Cioppino

Sometimes I think that if I could, I'd live underwater and eat fish all the time! If you feel the same way—or if you just like seafood—then I bet you'll go for this simple and delicious meal. It's full of good, healthy stuff—and it's all naturally low-carb. That said, seafood is expensive, so don't spend a fortune by buying more than you need. I usually ask the person behind the seafood counter to give me shellfish by the piece. If I only need 5 shrimp or 5 clams, then that's what I ask for! (It's easier to open a clamshell with your thumbnail than it is to get one of the Stellas to spend more than he has to!) Remember, low-carb doesn't have to be expensive.

YIELD:
4 servings

NET CARBOHYDRATES:
5.5 grams per serving

PREP:
20 minutes

COOK:
10 minutes

3 tablespoons Scampi Butter (page 88)
1 pound fish fillets, cut into 4 equal pieces (recommended: grouper, tilapia, mahi, snapper, or cod)
½ pound (8 to 10) peeled and deveined shrimp, with tails
½ pound sea scallops
15 ounces tomatoes, diced (canned tomatoes are fine, just be sure there's no added sugar)
1 pound mussels (approximately 20), scrubbed and debearded*
1 dozen small clams (you may use cherrystone or Ipswich steamers)
4 pieces snow crab claws, optional (you may use split legs, cut into 3-inch pieces)
2 tablespoons white wine
3 tablespoons fresh basil chiffonade,** plus 4 sprigs for garnish

1. Place the scampi butter in a large pan at least 2 inches deep and melt it over medium-high heat.

2. Add the fish, shrimp, and scallops. Cook for about 2 minutes, stirring the shrimp and scallops around in the pan and flipping the fish once.

3. Add the tomatoes, mussels, clams, and crab claws, then pour the white wine over everything.

4. Sprinkle with the basil chiffonade, cover, and cook for about 4 minutes, until the clams and mussels open. (Discard any that do not open.)

5. Remove from the heat. Divide the seafood evenly among 4 large, shallow soup or pasta bowls, then pour the liquid from the pan over all. Garnish each bowl with a sprig of basil.

*COOK'S TIP: To debeard a mussel, grab the exposed beard tightly and pull with an upward jerk to remove.

**COOK'S TIP: To create a chiffonade, make a stack of 4 or 5 basil leaves. Roll them up into a tight tube like a cigar. Then slice across the "cigar" to make slender ribbons of basil.

HELPFUL HINT

If you want a great, easy bread to serve with this cioppino, simply start with our pizza crust dough (page 58). Bake the crust at 375° F for 12 to 15 minutes, until lightly golden brown. Then sprinkle with grated Parmesan cheese, garlic powder, and salt and return to the oven for about a minute more until golden brown. You can even cut it into tiny triangles and serve them on top of the cioppino!

Vegetables

Of all the major food categories, vegetables seem to cause the most confusion among low-carbers. Some people think you're not allowed to eat any vegetables if you're low-carbing; others think you can eat all you want! (Of course they're both right, depending on which vegetable it is.)

Corn, carrots, potatoes, and most beans (which are technically legumes, not vegetables) are high in carbs, so I avoid them when I'm eating *Stella Style* (although soybeans and green beans are low-carb, and welcome). Asparagus, broccoli, cauliflower, cucumbers, jicama, mushrooms, celery, yellow squash, radishes, eggplant, zucchini, and peppers are all low in carbs and, therefore, perfect for eating *Stella Style* (as well as moderate amounts of tomatoes and onions). Pumpkins are great too; they're naturally low-carb and full of fiber! Olives of all kinds are **in** too, as are all herbs. And don't forget collard greens, mustard greens, and spinach.

One of the great things about grocery shopping today is how much more choice we have in the produce aisle; I never saw jicama or Jerusalem artichokes in those aisles when I was growing up in Florida! However, with all the choices you have today, it's hard to know what's high-carb and what's not. The best thing to do is look it up in a carbohydrate counter. You'll find them in the bookstores and on the web, so check one out

Garlic Mock Mashed Potatoes

Vegetables Casino

Grilled Summer Vegetables

Zucchini, Yellow Squash, and Tomato Fromage

Old-Fashioned Egg Mock Potato Salad

Deep-Fried Onion Rings

Jicama Matchstick Fries

Southern Green Beans and Pecans

Cilantro Vegetable Kebabs

Collard Greens and Roasted Peppers

Waldorf Cole Slaw

Cole Slaw

Sausage and Herb Stuffing

before you substitute any vegetables in these recipes. I definitely want you to be creative, but stay low-carb!

In the pages that follow, you'll learn how to make **Zucchini, Yellow Squash, and Tomato Fromage, Vegetables Casino,** and **Southern Green Beans and Pecans.** And don't forget that one of the most important principles of eating *Stella Style* is reinventing your old favorites, so even though potatoes are out, don't be surprised to see **Garlic Mock Mashed Potatoes** among the recipes in this section.

Your mom was right—you need to eat your vegetables. Just eat them *Stella Style!*

Garlic Mock Mashed Potatoes

The key to success when you're eating **Stella Style** is finding low-carb alternatives to your favorite high-carb foods—NOT doing without! That means "thinking outside the box." A perfect example is this recipe, which uses cauliflower to replace high-carb potatoes. Cauliflower has a neutral taste, and it does a terrific job of absorbing the flavor of the other ingredients in any recipe. Try this great side dish for family dinners, especially holidays—and with Wild Mushroom Turkey Gravy (page 80), of course!

1 medium head cauliflower
1 tablespoon cream cheese, softened
¼ cup grated Parmesan cheese
¼ teaspoon minced fresh garlic
 teaspoon chicken base or bouillon (you may substitute
    ½ teaspoon salt)
⅛ teaspoon freshly ground black pepper
½ teaspoon chopped fresh or dried chives, for garnish
3 tablespoons unsalted butter

> **YIELD:**
> 4 servings
>
> **NET CARBOHYDRATES:**
> 4 grams per serving
>
> **PREP:**
> 15 minutes
>
> **COOK:**
> 6 minutes

1. Bring a large pot of water to a boil over high heat.

1. Clean and cut the cauliflower into small pieces. Cook in the boiling water for about 6 minutes, until well done.

2. Drain well. Do not let cool. Pat the cooked cauliflower very dry between several layers of paper towels (otherwise your "potatoes" will fall apart).

3. With an immersion blender in a deep bowl or in a food processor, pulse the hot cauliflower with the cream cheese, Parmesan, garlic, chicken base, and pepper until almost smooth.

4. Garnish with chives and serve hot with pats of butter.

HELPFUL HINT

Try adding a little roasted garlic or chopped fresh rosemary for a whole new taste!

Vegetables Casino

Clams Casino is one of my all-time favorites (page 148), so one day I decided to try a veggie variation of that classic recipe. Everyone loved it—even the kids! Cooking vegetables doesn't get any easier than this, especially if you've already got the oven on. Just pop them in the oven about 12 minutes before the rest of the meal is done, and your whole meal will be ready all at once!

YIELD:
6 servings

NET CARBOHYDRATES:
9 grams per serving

PREP:
15 minutes

COOK:
12 minutes

Vegetable oil cooking spray
2 small eggplants
2 small to medium yellow squash
4 Roma tomatoes
Kosher salt
Freshly ground black pepper
Garlic powder
2 tablespoons real bacon bits (use imitation bacon bits if you're making a vegetarian meal)
1 tablespoon finely diced red bell pepper
1 tablespoon finely diced green bell pepper
1 tablespoon finely diced red onion
¾ cup grated Parmesan cheese
2 tablespoons extra-virgin olive oil

1. Preheat the oven to 350° F. Spray a small baking sheet with cooking spray.

2. Cut off the ends of both the eggplants and yellow squash and cut each lengthwise in half. Lay cut side up and close together on the baking sheet.

3. Cut the tops and a very small piece of the bottoms off the Roma tomatoes and stand them up next to the squash on the baking sheet.

4. Top with the diced vegetables.

5. Sprinkle all the vegetables liberally with salt, pepper, garlic powder, bacon bits, peppers, and onion.

6. Carefully sprinkle the Parmesan over every vegetable, piling the cheese high, then drizzle with olive oil. Bake for about 12 minutes, until the cheese starts to turn golden brown. Serve immediately.

HELPFUL HINT

You can also use this same method and toppings for chicken breast and fish! Just add a bit of lemon juice and white wine and bake or broil!

Grilled Summer Vegetables

You just don't hear enough about all the wonderful vegetables allowed on a low-carb plan. Whenever I fire up the grill, I open the fridge, grab all the veggies in sight, and throw them on too! Only after they're cooked do I start thinking about what I'll do with them (they usually end up in two or three different meals). This recipe is one we've enjoyed for years!

YIELD:
10 servings

NET CARBOHYDRATES:
6 grams per serving

PREP:
20 minutes

COOK:
10 minutes

1 medium yellow squash, halved lengthwise
1 medium zucchini, halved lengthwise
1 medium eggplant, sliced ½ inch thick
1 red onion, sliced ½ inch thick
2 Roma tomatoes, halved lengthwise
3 green onions (scallions)
1 red bell pepper, seeds removed, quartered into large
    flat pieces
1 yellow bell pepper, seeds removed, quartered into large
    flat pieces
2 portobello mushroom caps
Kosher salt
Freshly ground black pepper
½ cup extra-virgin olive oil
4 cloves garlic, minced

Special equipment: Grill

1. Preheat the grill to high.

2. Place all of the vegetables in a large bowl. Season generously with salt and pepper and toss with the olive oil and minced garlic.

3. Place the vegetables cut side down on the white-hot grill. Cook for only a couple minutes on each side until tender and nicely marked by the grill. Remove from the grill and serve immediately.

HELPFUL HINTS

Adding a little butter will really add to the vegetables' natural flavors. You can also cut the leftovers into bite-sized chunks and marinate them in Greek Dressing (page 94) or put them into an empty jar with leftover pickle juice. Mmm!

Zucchini, Yellow Squash, and Tomato Fromage

Tomato fromage is not only an easy-to-make vegetable dish but also a great garnish that appears frequently in French cuisine. Add a few healthy, colorful low-carb vegetables, like zucchini and yellow squash, and you'll be surprised how quickly everyone in the house will be coming back for more!

YIELD:
6 servings

NET CARBOHYDRATES:
2 grams per serving

PREP:
5 minutes

COOK:
12 minutes

Vegetable oil cooking spray
2 small to medium zucchini
2 small to medium yellow squash
4 Roma tomatoes
Kosher salt
Freshly ground black pepper
Garlic powder
¾ cup grated Parmesan cheese (more or less as desired)
1 tablespoon extra-virgin olive oil

1. Preheat the oven to 350° F. Spray a small baking sheet with cooking spray and set aside.

2. Cut off the ends of the zucchini and yellow squash, then cut each lengthwise in half. Place the pieces cut side up close together on the baking sheet.

3. Cut a small piece off the bottom of each tomato and stand them up on the same pan with the squash.

4. Sprinkle everything in the pan liberally with salt, pepper, and garlic powder.

5. Next carefully pile the Parmesan cheese high on every piece.

6. Drizzle the olive oil over the zucchini and squash (but not the tomatoes), then bake for about 12 minutes, until the squash and cheese start to turn golden brown.

7. Remove and serve while still warm.

Old-Fashioned Egg Mock Potato Salad

This is a reinvention of my mother's recipe that my family has enjoyed forever! Cauliflower has a neutral flavor that absorbs whatever you add to it, so it's a perfect alternative to potatoes. This is the best use of cauliflower—reinvented as potatoes—I've ever tasted, and once you've tasted it I know you'll agree!

1 large head cauliflower, cleaned and finely diced
     (about 4 cups)
6 hard-boiled large eggs, chopped
1 cup finely diced celery (2 ribs)
1 cup mayonnaise
½ teaspoon yellow table mustard
½ teaspoon freshly ground black pepper
¼ teaspoon kosher salt
⅛ teaspoon garlic powder
paprika, for garnish
minced fresh parsley for garnish

YIELD:
8 servings

NET CARBOHYDRATES:
2 grams per serving

PREP:
10 minutes

COOK:
10 minutes

CHILL:
1 hour

1. Set a large pot of water over high heat and bring to a boil.

2. Cook the cauliflower pieces in the boiling water for about 5 minutes, until tender. Drain thoroughly and immerse in an ice water bath to stop the cooking. Drain well, then pat dry between several layers of paper towels.

3. Place the cauliflower in a bowl with all the remaining ingredients except the paprika and parsley and mix well with a large kitchen spoon.

4. Sprinkle with the paprika and parsley, then chill for at least 1 hour before serving.

HELPFUL HINTS

This recipe is even better the next day! Try adding a tablespoon of chopped fresh dill for a completely different flavor!

Deep-Fried Onion Rings

Being able to eat your favorite fried foods on low-carb couldn't be simpler; you've just got to make one little change. When you're carb-proofing your pantry, just throw out your white flour and put soy flour in its place! If you're like me, you'll love these fried onion rings on top of a perfectly grilled steak!

YIELD:
12 servings

NET CARBOHYDRATES:
6 grams per serving

PREP:
20 minutes

COOK:
5 to 10 minutes

3 to 6 cups vegetable oil (more or less depending on
   pot size)
3 large eggs
¼ cup heavy cream or water

BREADING:
2⅓ cups soy flour
2 teaspoons salt
1 teaspoon freshly ground black pepper
1 teaspoon garlic powder
1 teaspoon poultry seasoning

3 large yellow onions

1. Place a deep, heavy pot over medium-high heat and fill with at least 1 inch vegetable oil. Heat the oil to 350° F; it's important to monitor and maintain the temperature or the breading and oil will burn. (Portable deep fryers are great for this, but if you don't have one, use a candy thermometer—just be careful!)

2. In a medium bowl, whisk the eggs and cream to make an egg wash.

3. In a larger bowl, mix the breading ingredients together.

4. Peel and slice the onions (be sure to cut thick slices), then carefully separate the rings. Dip each individual onion ring into the breading, then the egg wash, and then back into the breading again, making sure to coat well.

5. Pat off any excess breading and carefully place the rings in the hot oil, using a slotted spoon (wear mitts). Fry until golden brown and crisp, 1 to 2 minutes. Repeat in batches as necessary. Remove the onion rings when they're done, drain on paper towels, and serve immediately.

COOK'S TIP: Most soy flour is made from toasted soybeans and has already been cooked. Therefore, it cooks—and browns—faster than plain flour when frying. Watch the onion rings very carefully, since they can go from toasty golden to just plain toasted in no time flat!

Jicama Matchstick Fries

Jicama is a recent addition to our household. One day I felt the urge for a snack, so I fired up the deep fryer, sliced up a jicama root, and discovered **Stella Style** fries! With just a little everyday seasoning, they taste almost like BBQ potato chips!

YIELD:
4 servings

NET CARBOHYDRATES:
2.5 grams per serving

PREP:
10 minutes

COOK:
5 minutes

3 to 6 cups vegetable oil (more or less depending on pot size)
1 medium jicama, peeled
Salt
Onion powder
Garlic powder
Paprika

1. Place a deep, heavy pot over medium-high heat and fill with at least 1 inch vegetable oil. Heat the oil to 350° F. (Portable deep fryers are great for this, but if you don't have one, use a candy thermometer—just be careful!)

2. Very thinly slice the jicama, as you would a potato to make chips, then stack a few slices at time and cut them all into matchstick-sized pieces.

3. Carefully place the chips into the hot oil (use a slotted spoon and wear mitts) and fry until very crispy (just a few minutes will do). Cook in batches as necessary. Remove and drain on paper towels.

4. Sprinkle liberally with equal amounts of salt, onion and garlic powders, and paprika to taste. Toss to coat well and serve immediately.

HELPFUL HINT

Cut the jicama into large chunks to make home fries in place of potatoes!

Southern Green Beans and Pecans

This is the easiest and tastiest way I know to prepare green beans. There's something about sautéing them that really draws out the flavor. Steaming doesn't cut it with me with certain veggies, and I'm betting you'll agree once you try these Southern-style beauties! Mmmm!

1 pound fresh green beans, ends trimmed
4 ounces bacon, cut into small pieces
¼ cup pecan halves
1 roasted red pepper, cut into strips
⅛ teaspoon garlic powder
⅛ teaspoon freshly ground black pepper
Salt to taste
2 tablespoons butter

YIELD:
6 servings

NET CARBOHYDRATES:
3 grams per serving

PREP:
10 minutes

COOK:
15 minutes

1. Place a small pot of water over high heat and bring to a boil.

2. Drop the trimmed green beans into the boiling water and cook for about 5 minutes, until tender but still crisp.

3. While the green beans are cooking, brown the bacon and pecans in a large sauté pan over medium heat.

4. When the green beans are done, drain them and add them to the sauté pan.

5. Add the pepper strips, garlic powder, pepper, salt to taste, and butter. Sauté together for 2 minutes on high and serve.

COOK'S TIP: If you're going to cook the green beans ahead of time, cool them in ice water the minute they're done to stop them from cooking further. Drain them and refrigerate until you're ready to use them. Cooked green beans are perfect candidates for the freezer too!

Cilantro Vegetable Kebabs

These kebabs are an especially flavorful way to prepare and present grilled vegetables. They're great for backyard barbecues, pool parties, or lunch or dinner any day of the week. Put a skewer or two of these on your kids' plates, and you'll never have to beg them to eat their veggies again!

YIELD:
8 servings

NET CARBOHYDRATES:
4 grams per serving

PREP:
10 minutes

COOK:
10 minutes

2 large yellow squash
2 large zucchini
1 medium eggplant
1 red onion
2 Roma tomatoes (you may also use 16 cherry tomatoes)
1 red bell pepper
1 yellow bell pepper
½ teaspoon kosher salt
½ teaspoon freshly ground black pepper
½ teaspoon minced fresh garlic
¼ cup extra-virgin olive oil
¼ cup red wine vinegar
2 tablespoons chopped fresh cilantro

Special Equipment: Grill, indoor grill top, or grill pan
Eight 8-inch bamboo skewers

1. Soak the skewers in water for 30 minutes so that they don't burn on the grill. Preheat the grill to medium-high or use an indoor grill top or grill pan over high heat.

2. Cut the ends off the vegetables, clean the seeds out of the peppers, then slice them all into pieces about 2 inches square. (Try to cut all the vegetables the same size so they'll cook evenly. If you're using cherry tomatoes, leave them whole.)

3. Season the vegetables generously with salt and pepper and toss all with the garlic and olive oil. Thread alternating pieces of all the vegetables on each skewer to about 1 inch from the blunt end.

4. Place the kebabs on the edge of the grill with the bare part of the stick hanging off the edge away from the fire. Watch closely, since the skewers will cook very quickly. Turn the skewers to the next side before they begin to burn, continuing until all four sides are cooked. The kebabs will be done in just 7 to 10 minutes when they have grill marks on all sides.

5. Remove the kebabs from the grill, drizzle with the vinegar, and sprinkle with the chopped cilantro. Serve hot as a vegetable or cold as a salad.

HELPFUL HINT

For an exciting difference, leave out the cilantro and replace the red wine vinegar with balsamic vinegar! Wow! What a change in flavor!

Collard Greens and Roasted Peppers

Collards are a staple in the South—both Rachel and I grew up eating them. My sister Stephanie still cooks some of the best fresh collards in Florida, but it's a lot of work, and I just don't have the patience. That's why I use frozen collards in this recipe, season them like Steph does, and then call it a day! Quick and easy—that's *Stella Style* for me!

YIELD:
6 servings:

NET CARBOHYDRATES:
2.5 grams per serving

PREP:
10 minutes

COOK:
4 minutes

4 tablespoons unsalted butter
2 ounces Parma ham, finely diced, optional (you may also use crumbled bacon)
2 tablespoons diced red onion
1 jar (6½ ounces) roasted red peppers, drained and julienned
1 clove garlic, minced
One 1-pound bag frozen collard greens, thawed, chopped, and drained well
Juice of ½ lemon
Kosher salt and freshly ground black pepper to taste

1. Melt the butter in a sauté pan over medium-high heat. Add the ham, onion, roasted peppers, and garlic and sauté just until tender.

2. Add the collards and sprinkle with the lemon juice. Stir and toss over heat for about 4 minutes, until hot. Add salt and pepper to taste.

3. Remove from the heat and serve.

HELPFUL HINTS

Try this recipe with fresh or frozen spinach. Simply omit the Parma ham if you prefer a vegetarian dish.

Waldorf Cole Slaw

Rachel came up with this wonderfully clever cole slaw recipe by using the key flavors of traditional Waldorf salad. This recipe joins the long list of comfort foods that have made a low-carb comeback—***Stella Style!***

$\frac{1}{2}$ **cup sour cream**

$\frac{1}{3}$ **cup mayonnaise**

$\frac{1}{2}$ **cup sugar substitute (or less, depending on your taste)**

$\frac{1}{2}$ **cup coarsely chopped walnuts**

2 tablespoons red wine vinegar

12 ounces shredded green cabbage

4 ounces shredded red cabbage

1 teaspoon kosher salt

$\frac{1}{8}$ **teaspoon freshly ground black pepper**

$\frac{1}{4}$ **teaspoon ground nutmeg**

YIELD:
10 servings
NET CARBOHYDRATES:
3 grams per serving
PREP:
15 minutes
CHILL:
2 hours

1. Mix all ingredients together in a large bowl, tossing to combine. Chill for 2 hours before serving.

Cole Slaw

I'm putting this recipe in the book because Rachel made me do it. Really! I told her we already have one slaw recipe (for Waldorf Cole Slaw, page 195), and I didn't think we needed another. Rachel was very calm—at first—but as the "discussion" went on, she became slightly more passionate in her defense of this recipe. This cole slaw is totally different, she said, and she should know, since she wrote them both! She says this one is the more traditional version. (According to her, it's the combination of the two different vinegars that makes it unique.) I'm giving in. After all, what choice do I have? Since I married her, she's NEVER been wrong!

YIELD:
10 servings

NET CARBOHYDRATES:
3 grams per serving

PREP:
15 minutes

CHILL:
2 hours

¾ **cup mayonnaise**
⅓ **cup sugar substitute (more or less depending on your taste)**
2 **tablespoons red wine vinegar**
2 **tablespoons apple cider vinegar**
12 **ounces shredded green cabbage**
4 **ounces shredded red cabbage**
1 **teaspoon celery seeds**
1 **teaspoon kosher salt**
⅛ **teaspoon freshly ground black pepper**

1. Mix all ingredients, in a large bowl, tossing to combine. Chill for 2 hours before serving.

HELPFUL HINT

This cole slaw is great alongside Southern Fried Chicken (page 132) and Grilled Country-Style Pork Ribs with Bourbon Barbecue Sauce (page 120)!

Sausage and Herb Stuffing

Stuffing is commonly made with bread or croutons, which makes it off-limits to low-carbers. But it doesn't have to be made that way. There's nothing wrong—and everything right—with substituting chopped vegetables and Rachel's fabulous Zucchini Muffins to make up the missing bulk. So don't get stuffed. Try this recipe instead of all that bread!

4 Zucchini Muffins (page 33), cut into small croutons
12 ounces ground pork breakfast sausage
¼ cup chopped red onion
¼ cup finely chopped celery
2 large eggs
½ cup grated Parmesan cheese
1 tablespoon chopped fresh parsley
1 tablespoon ground sage
1 tablespoon dried thyme
1 clove garlic, minced
⅛ teaspoon salt
⅛ teaspoon freshly ground black pepper

Special equipment: 8 x 8-inch glass baking dish

YIELD:
8 servings

NET CARBOHYDRATES:
4 grams per serving

PREP:
15 minutes

COOK:
30 minutes

1. Preheat the oven to 350° F. While the oven is warming up, spread the muffin cubes on a baking sheet and place in the oven. Remove when the croutons are dry.

2. Brown the sausage with the onion and celery in a sauté pan over medium heat and drain off the excess fat with a spoon or turkey baster.

3. In a bowl, beat the eggs, then mix in all the stuffing ingredients along with the browned sausage.

4. Pour the mixture into the baking dish and bake for 30 minutes. Serve hot.

HELPFUL HINT

This is simply perfect for Thanksgiving dinner served with Wild Mushroom Turkey Gravy (page 80)!

Beverages

Water, of course, is the ultimate low-carb beverage—I try to drink six to eight glasses of water a day. I like plain tap water, fancy bottled fizzy water, and flavored and plain seltzer. I also enjoy any kind of diet soda—as long as it's made with sugar substitute, not those sodas that boast "half the calories," which means they've still got half the sugar. However, everyone needs a break from the same old beverages now and then. If it's a hot summer day, how about starting with Christian's **Lemon-Lime Slushee**? Or if you want to relax at the end of a long day at the office, how about an ice-cold **Strawberry Daiquiri**!

Alcohol can certainly be part of *Stella Style*, as long as we're talking low-carb. Hard liquors such as vodka, tequila, scotch, and bourbon all have zero carbs, but of course, that doesn't mean you should be drinking them all day—or night! (I'm a firm believer in moderation in drinking. Don't forget that drinking too much can lower your resistance to high-carb temptations.) Dry red and white wines are great for low-carbing (with only one or two carbs per glass), but steer clear of beer. Just one can of "regular" beer has about ten carbs, with some brands having twice that. And although the new breed of lite and low-carb beers have about half the carbs of regular beer, they are still made from barley and hops, which are not part of a low-carb lifestyle and may trip up your weight-loss efforts.

At any rate, drinking *Stella Style* is pretty much the same as eating *Stella Style*. Use your imagination to make low-carb recreations of your old favorites, but always let a friend drive if you've "recreated" one or two too many!

White Wine Spritzer

Sangria *Stella Style*

Mojitos

Lemon-Lime Slushees

Strawberry Milkshakes

Strawberry Daiquiris

White Wine Spritzers

Dry white wine has about one net carb per five-ounce glass, and the carbs come from natural sugar sources, which are always allowed in a low-carb lifestyle. Because of the natural sugars and because it's just good measure, moderation is the key.

YIELD:
8 servings

NET CARBOHYDRATES:
3 grams per serving

PREP:
10 minutes

2 cups dry white wine (we suggest Chablis, Chardonnay, or Sauvignon Blanc), chilled
2 cups diet lemon-lime soda (diet 7-Up, Sprite, or Fresca work well), chilled
¼ cup fresh lime juice (about 2 limes)
¼ cup fresh lemon juice (about 1 large lemon)
½ cup sugar substitute (Splenda recommended)
1 lemon, thinly sliced
1 lime, thinly sliced

1. Mix all the ingredients except the lemon and lime slices in a pitcher. Fill 8 glasses with ice and pour about ½ cup spritzer into each glass. Garnish with the lemon and lime slices and serve immediately.

Sangria *Stella Style*

This is a reinvention of a recipe that I learned to make while working in a Mexican restaurant in Florida. Back then, I thought there was no difference between wine, beer, or hard liquor, but I couldn't have been more wrong. A bottle of beer has about ten carbs—a glass of red wine, only two! So don't drink and drive, but by all means enjoy a glass or two of this delicious sangria—*Stella Style!*

2 cups burgundy wine
2 cups club soda or seltzer water (you may substitute diet
    lemon-lime soda)
¼ cup fresh lime juice (about 2 limes)
¼ cup fresh lemon juice (about 1 large lemon)
½ cup sugar substitute (Splenda recommended)
1 lemon, thinly sliced
1 lime, thinly sliced
¼ cup diet fruit drink, optional (we love all varieties of
    Crystal Light)

YIELD:
12 servings

NET CARBOHYDRATES:
3 grams per serving

PREP:
10 minutes

1. Mix all the ingredients together in a punch bowl. Refrigerate until ready to serve.

2. Fill 12 glasses with ice and pour the sangria over the ice to serve.

HELPFUL HINTS

Make the sangria as close to serving time as possible so it has plenty of fizz! You can also use this recipe with Champagne for a punch.

Mojito

If you're looking for a refreshing drink on a hot summer day, this popular Cuban classic will help cool you off! We were out with friends recently and everyone was drinking these—everyone but us, of course, because bartenders load them up with sugar. That night, as soon as we got home, we got right on it and reinvented this delicious summer cooler. *Muy bueno!*

YIELD:
4 servings, 8 ounces each

NET CARBOHYDRATES:
2.5 grams per serving

PREP:
10 minutes

Ice cubes (enough to fill a shaker)
5 ounces light rum
5 tablespoons fresh lime juice (about 3 limes)
10 sprigs fresh mint, torn apart, plus 4 sprigs for garnish
3 tablespoons sugar substitute (adjust according to taste)
4 tablespoons club soda
4 slices lime

1. Fill a drink shaker with the ice, rum, lime juice, torn mint, and sugar substitute. Shake vigorously and pour over ice in 4 highball glasses. Add a splash of club soda to each glass, then garnish with a sprig of mint and slice of lime on the edge of the glass.

HELPFUL HINT

Alcohol has been known to slow weight loss in some individuals on low-carb lifestyles. Rachel and I have always enjoyed a cocktail now and then, and it didn't slow our weight loss down, but we're all different. As in anything—even *Stella Style*—moderation is the key.

Lemon-Lime Slushees

We never pressured our boys into eating low-carb, they just kind of drifted into it on their own. At first they just picked at what was left after our meals, then slowly they began to show up around the time the food arrived on the table. After a while, as they saw the variety of food, they realized that we were still eating most everything we used to—to say nothing of things we had always been told to avoid. Getting into the spirit, Christian came up with this simple, low-carb summer cooler—and he still makes it today!

Juice of 2 lemons (about 3 ounces) (you may use
    reconstituted juice)
Juice of 2 limes (about ¼ cup)
¾ cup water
2 cups ice cubes
1 cup sugar substitute (Splenda recommended)
Lemon slices, for garnish
Lime slices, for garnish

YIELD:
8 servings

NET CARBOHYDRATES:
6 grams per serving

PREP:
5 minutes

1. Put all the ingredients in a blender or food processor, cover tightly, and blend on high for 1 to 2 minutes, until smooth. Pour into 4 glasses and garnish with fresh lemon and lime slices.

HELPFUL HINT

Use the pulse button to turn the blender on and off to help chop the ice evenly.

Strawberry Milkshakes

Rachel and I like this as a quick fix for the sugar itch! It's strange, but this shake just isn't as good made with fresh berries (unless you freeze them first). I think it's something about the way frozen berries blend into the cream! I won't even pretend that we know why, but when something so easy tastes sooo good, we just go with it!

YIELD:
4 servings, 8 ounces
each

NET CARBOHYDRATES:
4.5 grams per serving

PREP:
5 minutes

1 cup ice
½ cup heavy cream
1 cup frozen strawberries (do not defrost)
¼ cup sugar substitute (Splenda recommended)
½ teaspoon sugar-free vanilla extract

1. Put all the ingredients in a blender or food processor and pulse to chop and keep the ice and berries moving. Switch to high and blend until smooth. Serve immediately.

Strawberry Daiquiris

Strawberry daiquiris, usually so high in sugar, were a natural for us to reinvent *Stella Style*, since strawberries are the best low-carb fruit around, with less than one net carb each. Rachel had already discovered that frozen berries make a great slushee! I took her lead, added some rum, and created this fun drink that goes down smooth but still packs a punch. If you're driving, there's a two-drink maximum!

12 ounces frozen strawberries
⅓ cup sugar substitute (you may adjust to taste)
¼ cup light rum
1 tablespoon fresh lemon juice
6 sprigs fresh mint
6 slices lemon

YIELD:
6 servings, 6 ounces
each

NET CARBOHYDRATES:
2.5 grams per serving

PREP:
10 minutes

1. Put the frozen strawberries, sugar substitute, rum, and lemon juice in a blender or food processor and blend until smooth. You may need to add a bit more rum or water to thin it to desired consistency (or potency). Pour into 6 wine glasses and garnish each with a sprig of mint and a slice of lemon on the edge of the glass.

HELPFUL HINT

You can use fresh strawberries if you prefer, but for best results, cut the tops off and freeze them before you pop them in the blender.

Desserts

Desserts are surely the biggest challenge you'll face when you start low-carbing. In fact, people ask Rachel and me all the time how you can possibly eat desserts while living a low-carb lifestyle? The answer is short and sweet: sugar substitute.

In general, when you're eating *Stella Style,* we want you to choose your favorite sugar substitute. However, when you're baking desserts, we want you to be a little more particular. You should definitely look for a granular sugar substitute that can stand in for sugar measure for measure. For baking, we recommend Splenda because we think it performs the best when heated; it browns and caramelizes just like real sugar.

If you're a chocoholic like me or Rachel, you can breathe a sigh of relief—we'd never ask you to give up your favorite treat. Just make it *Stella Style!* We'll introduce you to our own recipe for low-carb *Stella Style* **Chocolate Chips**—much cheaper than the kind you buy in the store—and teach you how to make scrumptious **Chocolate Pecan Bon Bons**, **Chocolate Frosting**, and other treats so good you'll never miss the carbs. The secret is unsweetened chocolate (we like Baker's brand) and unsweetened cocoa powder. (Make sure you don't buy instant cocoa mix; even the no-sugar-added version is full of sugar!)

You'll see a lot of heavy cream, cream cheese, sour cream, ricotta cheese, and other dairy products in *Stella Style* desserts. Remember to use the full-fat versions of these; we never use "lite" anything because the low-calorie versions almost always take out the fat and put in high-carb filler instead. And forget about margarine; nothing beats the taste of real butter—and it's got no carbs.

Another secret to low-carb desserts is using soy flour instead of regular flour; it's much lower in carbs and higher in nutrients. Soy flour is available at larger grocery and health food stores. (We use Arrowhead Mills brand.) If you don't bake a lot and won't be using the soy flour often, store it in your refrigerator or freezer, since it will go bad more quickly than regular flour.

Finally, remember that sugar lurks in a lot of baking extracts like vanilla and almond. We've found that most generic brands of common extracts used in cooking (like vanilla and almond extracts) don't come with added sugars, but that's not true across the board, so be sure to **check the labels**!

Stella Style Chocolate Chips

Sometimes you can't find low-carb ingredients you can trust. Some of the low-carb chocolate bars or candies on the market today list a whopping sixty-five carbs but somehow, after a sea of ingredients, end up with zero "net" carbs. Statements like that worry me, so I recommend you make these simple chocolate chips so you'll KNOW what you're getting! Sometimes, it's the little things that count! You'll want these delicious chips around to make many of your favorite desserts—*Stella Style!* You can use them for our Chocolate Chip Muffins (page 34), our Cannoli Parfaits (page 230), and lots of other recipes.

1 ounce unsweetened chocolate, chopped (we use Baker's)
½ cup sugar substitute (Splenda recommended)
2 tablespoons heavy cream or butter

1. Place the unsweetened chocolate in a heatproof bowl and melt over a saucepan of simmering water.

2. Whisk in the sugar substitute, then thin with the cream or butter. Whisk to blend thoroughly. Remove from the heat, spread on a plate covered with waxed paper, and freeze for about 15 minutes.

3. Break into small chunks after chilling to use in your favorite recipes!

YIELD:
½ cup

NET CARBOHYDRATES:
4 grams per serving

PREP:
10 minutes

COOK:
5 minutes

FREEZE:
15 minutes

Chocolate Pecan Brownies with Cream Cheese Frosting

These decadently rich brownies will definitely keep you satisfied, and that's what *Stella Style* is all about. Not having to do without desserts like this helped us succeed in reaching our weight loss goals! (And for those of you who are just visiting, and don't need to lose weight, they're just plain good!)

YIELD:
25 servings

NET CARBOHYDRATES:
4 grams per serving

PREP:
30 minutes

COOK:
40 minutes

Vegetable oil cooking spray
1½ tablespoons wheat or oat bran
1¼ cups plus 1½ teaspoons soy flour
4 ounces unsweetened baking chocolate (we use Baker's)
½ cup (1 stick) unsalted butter
2 cups sugar substitute (Splenda recommended)
½ cup heavy cream
5 large eggs
1 tablespoon sugar-free vanilla extract
2 teaspoons baking powder
½ cup chopped pecans
Cream Cheese Frosting (page 233)

Special equipment: 8-inch square baking pan

1. Place the rack in the center of the oven and preheat to 325° F. Spray the baking pan with cooking spray.

2. Mix the bran and 1½ teaspoons soy flour together and sprinkle evenly over the inside of the greased pan, also coating the sides.

3. Place the chocolate and butter in a heatproof bowl and melt over a saucepan of simmering water. Whisk in 1 cup of the sugar substitute and ¼ cup of the cream. Once it is thoroughly blended, remove from the heat.

4. With an electric mixer on high, beat the eggs, remaining 1 cup sugar substitute, and the vanilla extract just until blended.

5. Reduce the speed to low and blend in the chocolate mixture. Turn off the mixer.

6. Use a spoon to mix in the baking powder, remaining 1¼ cups soy flour, the pecans, and remaining ¼ cup cream.

7. Spread the batter evenly in the prepared pan and bake for 35 to 40 minutes, until a toothpick inserted in the center comes out clean. (Do not overbake or the brownies will be dry and hard.) Cool completely before frosting. Cut into 5 rows by 5 rows to make 25 pieces.

HELPFUL HINTS

We keep these brownies refrigerated because we love the way they taste cold, probably because they have cream cheese frosting. You may like them warm; it's your choice! They'll keep for 5 days in the refrigerator.

Chocolate Macadamia Nut Ice Cream

Quick, easy-to-make desserts are a very important part of living **Stella Style** (because you have to be able to whip them up whenever the urge strikes you)! It was easy to reinvent ice cream but the real challenge was creating a low-carb version that didn't take hours to make. Well, this recipe sure solves that problem—**Stella Style!**

YIELD:
4 servings

NET CARBOHYDRATES:
4 grams per serving

PREP:
15 minutes

COOK:
7 minutes

CHILL:
30 to 60 minutes

1 cup heavy cream
½ cup sugar substitute (Splenda recommended)
1 teaspoon sugar-free vanilla extract
⅛ teaspoon sugar-free almond extract
1 tablespoon unsweetened cocoa powder (not instant cocoa mix)
2 tablespoons ricotta cheese
¼ cup coarsely chopped macadamia nuts
Stella Style Whipped Cream, for garnish, optional (page 231)
4 strawberries, cut into fans, for garnish, optional
1 teaspoon unsweetened cocoa powder, for garnish, optional
4 fresh sprigs mint, for garnish, optional

Special equipment: 4 champagne glasses (coupes, not flutes, since they have to stand upright in the freezer)

1. With an electric mixer on high, whip the cream in a bowl just until frothy. Add the sugar substitute, extracts, cocoa powder, and ricotta cheese and beat on high speed until soft peaks form. Be careful not to overwhip it, or the cream will break down.

2. Use a spoon or spatula to fold in most of the macadamia nuts (save a few for garnish).

3. Using a 3-ounce ice cream scoop, place 1 scoop in each champagne glass and freeze for 1 hour to make mock ice cream, or refrigerate for 30 minutes if serving as a

parfait. If desired, garnish with whipped cream, reserved macadamia nuts, strawberry fans, cocoa powder, mint sprigs, or all of the above!

HELPFUL HINT

If the frozen "ice cream" is too hard to eat, take it out of the freezer for a couple minutes before serving.

Chocolate Ganache

You can still have chocolate on low-carb—as long as it's prepared **Stella Style,** which makes it taste like a cross between dark and semisweet chocolate. This recipe is made from real chocolate, just like our **Stella Style** Chocolate Chips (page 209), and its uses are limited only by your imagination!

YIELD:
4 servings

NET CARBOHYDRATES:
4 grams per serving

PREP:
10 minutes

COOK:
5 minutes

1 ounce unsweetened chocolate, chopped (we use Baker's)
½ cup sugar substitute (Splenda recommended)
2 tablespoons heavy cream or butter

1. Place the unsweetened chocolate in a heatproof bowl to melt over a pot of simmering water. (Be careful not to let the water boil rapidly, or the chocolate might burn.)

2. Whisk in the sugar substitute, then thin with the cream or butter, adding a little bit at a time and blending thoroughly after each addition. You may use less than the full 2 tablespoons or a bit more, depending on the consistency you desire.

3. Turn the heat off and leave the bowl resting over the hot water if you want to use the chocolate while it's still warm for dipping fresh fruits. If you prefer, scrape it into a container, cover, and refrigerate for use in a variety of dessert recipes.

HELPFUL HINT

You may reheat the ganache whenever you need it; simply rewarm it over a pot of simmering water. I don't recommend microwaving it, as it burns or seizes easily.

Chocolate Pecan Bon Bons

One night, way back when, my creative juices were really flowing (encouraged by some candy craving). Whew! That was a mouthful, and so are these "feel-like-you're-cheating," low-carb candy treats!

¼ **cup chopped pecans**
2 tablespoons sugar substitute (Splenda recommended)
½ **teaspoon sugar-free vanilla extract**
4 ounces cream cheese
Chocolate Ganache (page 214)

1. Using a fork, mix the pecans, sugar substitute, and vanilla into the cream cheese until well blended.

2. Form the mixture into small marble-sized balls. Line a dish that will fit into your freezer with waxed paper and place the balls in a single layer on the dish. Freeze the balls for at least 20 minutes.

3. While they're chilling, prepare the Chocolate Ganache.

4. Dip the frozen pecan cream cheese balls one at a time into the warm chocolate (otherwise the ganache will cool down and begin to harden). Remove each cream cheese ball as soon as it's coated and put it back on the waxed paper. Once all the cream cheese balls have been coated with chocolate, use a fork to spread them on the plate so that none of them are touching. Freeze for a few minutes until the chocolate has hardened. Serve the bon bons frozen but eat them quickly before they melt! These treats DO melt in your hand, as well as your mouth!

YIELD:
12 servings

NET CARBOHYDRATES:
4.5 grams per serving

PREP:
15 minutes

FREEZE:
25 minutes

COOK:
10 minutes

Stella Style New York Ricotta Cheesecake

Created out of necessity, this utterly decadent and satisfying dessert saved us from giving in to our sugar cravings so many times I've lost count! After years of loving trial and error, Rachel created the ultimate low-carb cheesecake. But be careful—once anyone tries this cheesecake, they'll be asking you to make it over and over again. We have to take one everywhere we go—or else!

YIELD:
12 servings

NET CARBOHYDRATES:
7 grams per serving

PREP:
30 minutes

COOK:
1¾ hours

COOL AND CHILL:
6 hours

Vegetable oil cooking spray
24 ounces cream cheese, softened
1 cup extra-fine ricotta cheese (process in a food processor for 1 minute)
½ cup sour cream
1½ cups sugar substitute (Splenda recommended)
⅓ cup heavy cream
1 tablespoon sugar-free vanilla extract
1 tablespoon fresh lemon juice
2 large eggs
3 large egg yolks (save the whites to make a great omelet later)

Special equipment: 8-inch springform cake pan*

1. Place the rack in the center of the oven and preheat to 400° F. Spray the springform pan with cooking spray.

2. Make a water bath so the top of the cheesecake won't split as it bakes: Pour about 1 inch water into a shallow roasting pan big enough to fit the cake pan and place it on the center rack of the oven to heat.

3. With an electric mixer on low speed, beat the cream cheese, ricotta, sour cream, and sugar substitute for about 1 minute, until well blended.

4. In a separate bowl, whisk the cream, vanilla, lemon juice, eggs, and egg yolks until blended.

5. Turn the mixer on medium speed and slowly pour the egg mixture into the cream cheese mixture. Beat just until blended; be careful not to overwhip.

6. Pour the batter into the greased springform pan. Place the pan in the heated water bath. Bake for 15 minutes, then lower the oven temperature to 275° F. Continue baking for 1½ hours, until the top is light golden brown and the cake is pulling away from the sides of the pan. Turn the oven off and leave the cake in the oven to cool for 3 hours. (This will keep the cake nice and tall.) Then remove the cake and refrigerate for at least 3 hours. Cut the cake into 12 slices before serving.

*COOK'S TIP: If you have trouble with a leaky springform pan, wrap the outside of the pan tightly with foil before placing it in the water bath.

HELPFUL HINT

Although all berries are part of eating *Stella Style,* strawberries are the lowest in carbs, with less than 1 carb per medium berry—and they're great on top of this cheesecake!

Key Lime Cheesecake

Rachel invented this cheesecake recipe when we first started eating low-carb. This easy no-bake version has always been one of our television audience's favorites!

YIELD:
12 servings

NET CARBOHYDRATES:
8 grams per serving

PREP:
20 minutes

CHILL:
3 to 4 hours

1 tablespoon wheat germ

2 cups plus 1 tablespoon sugar substitute (Splenda recommended)

16 ounces cream cheese, at room temperature

1 cup sour cream

1 cup ricotta cheese

¾ cup Key lime juice (you may use any fresh or bottled juice, but check the label to make sure it has no added sugars!)

2 tablespoons sugar-free vanilla extract

¼ cup hot water

Grated zest of 2 limes

3 envelopes unflavored gelatin (we prefer Knox)

¾ cup boiling water

Special equipment: 10-inch pie plate or cake pan

1. Sprinkle the wheat germ and 1 tablespoon sugar substitute over the bottom of the pie plate to create a mock crust.

2. With an electric mixer on medium speed, beat together the cream cheese, sour cream, ricotta, lime juice, remaining 2 cups sugar substitute, vanilla extract, hot water, and zest of 1 lime until well blended.

3. In a separate bowl, thoroughly dissolve the gelatin in the boiling water, using a fork to mix. Do not let cool and move immediately to the next step. (It's very important that the water be boiling hot and that you quickly mix the gelatin so it dissolves quickly. Otherwise, you'll end up with lumps.)

4. With the mixer on high—and working very quickly so the gelatin does not set— blend the hot, dissolved gelatin thoroughly into the cheesecake mixture.

5. Immediately pour the mixture into the prepared pie pan and sprinkle with the zest of the other lime. Refrigerate for 3 to 4 hours until firm. Cut into 12 slices and serve.

HELPFUL HINT

If there's extra cheesecake mixture left over after filling the pie pan (and I always seem to have more than I need), just put it into a pastry bag fitted with a decorating tip or a heavy-duty plastic bag with one corner snipped off. Freeze for 7 to 10 minutes, until it reaches the thickness of whipped cream. Once it's ready, use it to decorate the top of the cheesecake, then put the cake back in the fridge to finish chilling.

Pumpkin Cheesecake

Rachel just can't stop inventing cheesecakes, and now this is the one we bring to relatives during the holidays! The combination of the pumpkin with the creamy cheesecake is indescribably delicious! I think it tastes like the best pumpkin pie in the world! Or is it the best cheesecake? You decide!

YIELD:
12 servings

NET CARBOHYDRATES:
8 grams per serving

PREP:
30 minutes

COOK:
2 hours

COOL AND CHILL:
6 hours

Vegetable oil cooking spray
24 ounces cream cheese, softened
1 cup extra-fine ricotta cheese (process in a food processor for about 1 minute)
One 15-ounce can pure pumpkin (NOT pumpkin pie filling)
1¾ cups sugar substitute (Splenda recommended)
5 teaspoons pumpkin pie spice*
⅓ cup heavy cream
1 tablespoon sugar-free vanilla extract
3 large eggs
3 large egg yolks (put the whites aside for an omelet)

Special equipment: 8-inch springform cake pan**

1. Place the rack in the center of the oven and preheat to 400° F. Spray the springform pan with cooking spray and set aside.

2. Make a water bath so the top of the cheesecake won't split as it bakes: Pour about 1 inch water in a shallow roasting pan big enough to fit the cake pan and place it in the oven to heat.

3. With an electric mixer on low speed, beat the cream cheese, ricotta, pumpkin, sugar substitute, and pumpkin pie spice for about 2 minutes until well blended.

4. In a separate bowl, whisk the cream, vanilla, eggs, and egg yolks until blended.

5. Turn the mixer on medium speed and slowly pour the egg mixture into the cream cheese mixture. Beat just until blended. Be careful not to overwhip.

6. Pour the batter into the greased springform pan. Place the pan in the heated water bath.

7. Bake for 15 minutes, then lower the oven temperature to 275° F. Continue baking for 2 hours, until the top of the cheesecake is light golden brown and the cake is pulling away from the sides of the pan. Turn the oven off when the cheesecake has finished cooking and leave the cake in the oven to cool for 3 hours. (This will keep the cake nice and tall.)

8. Remove the cake from the oven and refrigerate for at least 3 hours. Cut into 12 slices and serve.

*COOK'S TIP: If you ever run out of pumpkin pie spice, you can simply make your own: Just shake together 3 tablespoons ground cinnamon, 1½ tablespoons ground ginger, 1 tablespoon ground nutmeg, and 2 teaspoons ground allspice. Store in an empty spice bottle on the shelf with your other spices.

**COOK'S TIP: If you have trouble with a leaky springform, wrap the outside tightly in foil before putting it in the water bath.

HELPFUL HINT

Serve with *Stella Style* Whipped Cream (page 231) for a rich delight!

Praline Pumpkin Pie

Depriving yourself during the holidays of all those wonderful traditional desserts and treats can be downright depressing, especially when everyone around you is pigging out.

We wouldn't want you to miss out on everyone's favorite, pumpkin pie—so here's Rachel's delectable rendition of an old classic. All our friends and family love it, and we make it for many different holidays throughout the year. Bring one with you to your next holiday get-together and you'll start a NEW holiday tradition in your family! (These pies freeze nicely, so make a few batches now to stock up for the requests!)

YIELD:
12 servings

NET CARBOHYDRATES:
6 grams per serving

PREP:
25 minutes

COOK:
1¼ hours

COOL AND CHILL:
3½ hours

PRALINE CRUST:
2 tablespoons butter
½ cup finely chopped pecans
½ cup sugar substitute (Splenda recommended)
⅛ teaspoon salt
⅛ teaspoon ground cinnamon

PIE FILLING:
One 15-ounce can pure pumpkin (NOT pumpkin pie filling)
¾ cup sugar substitute (Splenda recommended)
1 tablespoon plus a dash more pumpkin pie spice*
1¼ cups heavy cream
4 large eggs

Special equipment: 10-inch deep-dish pie pan

1. Preheat the oven to 350° F.

2. Make the crust: Melt the butter in a small saucepan or in the microwave and mix all the crust ingredients together in a small bowl.

3. While the mixture is still warm from the butter, press it evenly over the bottom of the pie pan (not the sides). Bake for about 5 minutes, until browned. Remove the crust from the oven. Turn the oven up to 425° F.

4. Make the filling: Place all the filling ingredients in a medium bowl and whisk together.

5. Pour the filling into the crust. Bake for 15 minutes, then reduce the oven heat to 350° F. Continue to bake for an additional 50 to 55 minutes until done. (To test for doneness, stick a toothpick in the center; if it comes out clean, the pie is done.) Cool on the counter for at least 30 minutes, then chill for at least 3 hours before serving. Try serving with a dollop of *Stella Style* Whipped Cream (page 231).

*COOK'S TIP: If you ever run out of pumpkin pie spice, you can simply make your own: Just shake together 3 tablespoons ground cinnamon, 1½ tablespoons ground ginger, 1 tablespoon ground nutmeg, and 2 teaspoons ground allspice together. Store in an empty spice bottle on the shelf with your other spices.

HELPFUL HINT

Pure pumpkin still has about 3 grams sugar per serving, but that's okay because the sugar is from a natural source.

Strawberries and Cream Parfaits

Plant City, Florida, is one of the strawberry capitals of the world, and for years we lived just down the road! On almost any street corner you could buy fresh strawberries for as low as five dollars a flat (twelve pints)! Well, if you think we loved strawberries then, imagine how we felt about them when we started low-carbing and found out that they're less than one net carb each! This recipe is a classic, yet simple, way to use this great low-carb berry.

YIELD:
4 servings

NET CARBOHYDRATES:
7 grams per serving

PREP:
20 minutes

CHILL:
30 minutes

1 cup heavy cream
$\frac{1}{3}$ cup sugar substitute
1 teaspoon sugar-free vanilla extract
2 pints fresh strawberries, sliced* (reserve a few for garnish)
Fresh mint sprigs, for garnish

Special equipment: 4 parfait glasses

1. With an electric mixer on high speed, whip the cream just until frothy. Add the sugar substitute and vanilla. Continue to whip until soft peaks form. Be careful not to overwhip, or the cream will break down.

2. In each of the parfait glasses, layer a couple spoonfuls of whipped cream, some fresh strawberry slices, a couple more spoonfuls of fresh whipped cream, and more strawberry slices. Chill for 30 minutes before serving. Garnish with a strawberry fan, sprig of fresh mint, and a dollop of the whipped cream if desired.

*COOK'S TIP: If the strawberries aren't naturally sweet enough for your taste, you may sprinkle them with an additional tablespoon of sugar substitute.

HELPFUL HINTS

You may freeze these parfaits for a great mock ice cream treat! Or try using fresh raspberries, blackberries, and blueberries. They're all great for eating *Stella Style!*

Strawberry Shortcake Martinis

This is another of Rachel's fabulous creations, and just one more example of the versatility of *Stella Style!* It uses her Zucchini Muffin recipe, an incredibly convenient, satisfying, and versatile muffin that can be served for dinner as well as dessert! Although Rachel and I have demonstrated this recipe in front of audiences for years, we're not even close to being tired of it. After all, we get to eat a few ourselves at the end of every demonstration!

2 pints strawberries, sliced
¼ cup sugar substitute (Splenda recommended)
12 Zucchini Muffins (page 33)
12 tablespoons *Stella Style* Whipped Cream (page 231)
1 pint whole strawberries, for garnish
12 sprigs fresh mint, for garnish

Special equipment: 12 martini glasses

1. Combine the sliced strawberries and sugar substitute and refrigerate for at least 30 minutes to allow the flavors to blend.

2. Cut the muffins horizontally in half (make sure they're cool if you've just baked them). Place each muffin bottom in a martini glass, then top with about ⅓ cup of the strawberry mixture.

3. Place the muffin tops on the strawberry filling. Garnish the "martinis" with whipped cream, whole berries, and mint sprigs.

HELPFUL HINTS

For best results, don't make the whipped cream until you're ready to serve this dish so it won't break down. You can try this same recipe with blueberries, raspberries, blackberries, or all of the above!

YIELD:
12 servings
NET CARBOHYDRATES:
10 grams per serving
PREP:
35 minutes
COOK:
25 minutes
CHILL:
30 minutes

Strawberry Gratin

I made my first incarnation of this recipe back in 1983 at Café Max in Pompano Beach, Florida. Our customers loved it then, and I know you'll love it now, because it's absolutely delicious and as easy as pie to make! No, come to think about it, it's much easier to make, just as good, and sooo much better for you! Since strawberries have less than one net carb each, you can indulge without guilt! Kids love this one too—they say it tastes just like ice cream. Go figure—it's served warm, like a cobbler!

YIELD:
8 servings

NET CARBOHYDRATES:
7 grams per serving

PREP:
12 minutes

COOK:
3 minutes

2 pints fresh strawberries, hulled, cut into quarters
¼ cup plus 1 tablespoon sugar substitute (Splenda recommended)
1 cup sour cream
1 tablespoon brown sugar substitute, optional*
Fresh mint sprigs, for garnish

1. Preheat the broiler to high and position the oven rack at the highest level.

2. Place the sliced berries in a sauté pan small enough to fit them tightly in a single layer and attractive enough to be used for serving.

3. Sprinkle the berries with 1 tablespoon sugar substitute, then cover with a thick, even layer of sour cream, leaving a ½-inch margin around the edges of the pan so the berries peek out.

4. Sprinkle the remaining ¼ cup sugar substitute evenly over the top, then sprinkle the brown sugar substitute, if using, over the top.

5. Place the pan under the broiler, keeping the oven door open and the handle of the pan sticking out. Broil for about 3 minutes, until the top just barely caramelizes. Watch carefully; if the sugar substitute starts to burn, remove the pan from the oven immediately. Serve warm, garnished with fresh mint.

*COOK'S TIP: If you can't find a brown sugar substitute such as Sugar Twin, simply omit this ingredient; it's only used to brown the top for color.

HELPFUL HINT

Go ALL OUT and make this recipe with an assortment of your favorite berries!

Neapolitan Parfaits

Heavy cream is a great appetite appeaser, so recipes like this will help you get through your sugar and dessert cravings. You can pull this dessert together quickly and pop it in the fridge to chill before you sit down to eat. When you get the urge for something sweet after dinner, it's already there waiting for you! Remember: **Stella Style** is all about planning ahead! Finally, don't forget that a small amount of cream more than doubles its volume when whipped, so don't overdo. In this case, a little truly goes a long way!

YIELD:
4 servings

NET CARBOHYDRATES:
7 grams per serving

PREP:
20 minutes

CHILL:
1 hour

1 cup heavy cream
⅓ cup plus 2 tablespoons sugar substitute
   (Splenda recommended)
1 teaspoon sugar-free vanilla extract
1½ teaspoons unsweetened cocoa powder (not cocoa mix)
1 pint fresh strawberries, sliced (sprinkle with
   1 tablespoon sugar substitute if they're not
   sufficiently sweet)
4 whole strawberries, for garnish
4 sprigs fresh mint, for garnish

Special equipment: 4 parfait glasses

1. With an electric mixer on high speed, whip the heavy cream just until frothy. Add ⅓ cup sugar substitute and the vanilla and whip just a little more to blend. Do not whip all the way to soft peaks yet.

2. Put half of the cream mixture into another bowl and whip it on high speed until stiff peaks form. Be careful not to overwhip, or the cream will break down. This is the vanilla cream. Set aside for later.

3. Add the cocoa powder and 2 tablespoons sugar substitute to the remaining half of the cream mixture, then whip on high speed until stiff peaks form (again being careful not to overwhip). This is the chocolate cream.

4. In each of the 4 parfait glasses, layer a couple spoonfuls of chocolate cream, some fresh strawberry slices, and a couple spoonfuls of vanilla cream. Refrigerate for 1 hour.

5. Cut the 4 strawberries into fans. Garnish each parfait with a strawberry fan and a sprig of fresh mint.

HELPFUL HINT

Try freezing the parfaits for a delicious ice cream!

Cannoli Parfaits

I come from an Italian family, and as far as we're concerned, cannolis are one of the major food groups! Since real cannolis are made from fresh, low-carb ingredients anyway, we decided to reinvent this one as soon as we started eating *Stella Style!* You'll never miss the pastry shell when you dive into these cannolis!

YIELD:
4 servings

NET CARBOHYDRATES:
7 grams per serving

PREP:
20 minutes

COOK:
5 minutes

CHILL:
1 hour

1 cup heavy cream
⅓ cup sugar substitute (Splenda recommended)
1 teaspoon sugar-free vanilla extract
¼ teaspoon sugar-free almond extract
⅓ cup ricotta cheese
One recipe *Stella Style* Chocolate Chips (page 209)

Special equipment: 4 parfait glasses

1. With an electric mixer on high speed, whip the cream just until frothy. Add the sugar substitute and extracts. Whip on high speed until soft peaks form. Be careful not to overwhip, or the whipped cream will break down.

2. Use a spoon to gently fold in the ricotta cheese and most of the chocolate chips, saving a few for garnish.

3. Spoon the cannoli cream into 4 parfait glasses, top with the remaining chocolate chips, and refrigerate for at least 1 hour before serving.

HELPFUL HINT

You can also freeze this dessert for a quick ice cream treat!

Stella Style Whipped Cream

Whipped cream is the perfect sweet treat for a low-carb lifestyle! A very small amount whips up into a filling and satisfying dessert! Because heavy whipping cream is naturally very sweet, you can even make this recipe without any sugar substitute at all! The fat content in the cream also works to stop cravings in their tracks, so don't be afraid to indulge once in a while. Eating *Stella Style* is NOT about doing without. This is an easy treat you can whip up late at night to top sugar-free Jell-O or to dip strawberries into to cure those munchies!

1 cup heavy cream
⅛ cup sugar substitute (Splenda recommended)
1 teaspoon sugar-free vanilla extract

1. With an electric mixer on high speed whip the heavy cream until frothy. Add the sugar substitute and extract and whip on high speed until soft peaks form. Be careful not to overwhip, or the cream will break down. Store leftovers in a pastry bag or glass dish with a lid and refrigerate.

YIELD:
12 servings

NET CARBOHYDRATES:
1 gram per serving

PREP:
10 minutes

Chocolate Frosting

At last, all the chocolate flavor and sweetness you could ever want but without the sugar! This frosting is great on everything from muffins to your index finger!

YIELD:
25 servings, 1 teaspoon per serving

NET CARBOHYDRATES:
1 gram per serving

PREP:
10 minutes

3 tablespoons unsalted butter, softened (not melted)

5 tablespoons unsweetened cocoa powder (not instant cocoa)

1 cup sugar substitute (Splenda recommended)

⅓ cup heavy cream

1 teaspoon sugar-free vanilla extract

Several drops hot water, as needed, to thin consistency

1. Place all the ingredients in a medium bowl and whisk until well blended. Thin with hot water, if necessary.

HELPFUL HINT

When you're frosting brownies, muffins, cakes, or other baked goods, make sure they're completely cooled, or the butter in the frosting will melt.

Cream Cheese Frosting

Cream cheese is a great low-carb staple! Even small amounts of it do a great job of appeasing hunger. Frosting made from cream cheese will bring out the flavor of low-carb baked goods from muffins to brownies—and help you cure your dessert cravings! This is just one of the many ways for you to be livin' low-carb and lovin' it!

8 ounces cream cheese, softened
¾ cup sugar substitute (Splenda recommended)
1 teaspoon sugar-free vanilla extract

1. Place all ingredients in a medium bowl and whisk until well blended.

HELPFUL HINT

When you're frosting brownies, muffins, cakes, or other baked goods, make sure they're completely cooled, or the frosting will melt.

YIELD:
25 servings; 1 teaspoon per serving

NET CARBOHYDRATES:
1 gram

PREP:
10 minutes

Index

alcohol consumption, 199, 202

almonds:

    in nutty muddy trail mix, 52

    in Renee's roasted cinnamon candied nuts, 51

American cheese, in stuffed meat loaf rollatini variation, 103

Anaheim shrimp scampi, 144

Anthony's pork chops Parmesan, 122

antipasto platter, last-minute, 70–71

appetizers, 61–77

artichokes, in last-minute antipasto platter, 70–71

Asiago cheese:

    in Anaheim shrimp scampi, 144

    in last-minute antipasto platter, 70–71

asparagus, in kitchen sink quiche, 46–47

Atkins Diet, 8–10

    Stella Style vs., 9–10, 14

avocados:

    in Anaheim shrimp scampi, 144

    in guacamole, 63

bacon:

    in BLT roll-ups, 64

    chicken with tomato, thyme and, 130–31

    in collard greens and roasted peppers, 194

    in kitchen sink quiche, 46–47

    in mock stuffed baked potato, 117

    in Southern green beans and pecans, 191

    in stuffed meat rollatini variation, 103

baked ham with maple bourbon glaze, 118–19

bald calzone, 160

bamboo shoots:

    in Szechuan vegetable stir-fry, 152–53

    in vegetable egg foo yung, 156–57

banana macadamia muffins, George's gorgeous, 32

barbecue sauce, no-cook bourbon, *see* bourbon barbecue sauce, no-cook

basil:

    in chicken with bacon, tomato, and thyme variation, 131

    in frittata Italiana, 42–43

    in last-minute antipasto platter, 70–71

    in mussels kimchee, 150

    in seafood cioppino, 176–77

beans, *see* specific beans

bean sprouts, in Szechuan vegetable stir-fry, 152–53

beef:

in Szechuan vegetable stir-fry variation, 153

in vegetable egg foo yung variation, 157

see also chuck, ground; steak

beef, ground:

in Claire's stuffed pumpkin, 108–9

in meat lasagna, 114–15

in stuffed cabbage, 104–5

in stuffed peppers, 110

beef tenderloin, Gorgonzola, 112–13

bell peppers:

in black soy bean chili, 98–99

in chili turkey burgers, 134–35

in cilantro vegetable kebabs, 192–93

in Gram's stuffed eggplant, 106–7

in grilled summer vegetables, 184–85

in Key West Caesar salad, 162–63

in low-carb pizza, 58–59

in minute steak salad, 168

in pico de gallo, 91

in stuffed meat loaf rollatini, 102–3

in stuffed peppers, 110

in Szechuan vegetable stir-fry, 152–53

in three-cheese veggie quesadillas, 154–55

in vegetable soufflé, 158–59

beverages, 199–205

blackberries:

in Rachel's raspberry muffins variation, 39

in strawberry shortcake martinis, variation, 225

blackened sea scallops with spinach and black soy beans, 142–43

blackening spice, 90

in blackened sea scallops with spinach and black soy beans, 142–43

in "if you had wings" chicken wings, 73

in remoulade sauce, 87

black soy bean chili, 98–99

in Ginny's taco salad, 171

black soy beans, blackened sea scallops with spinach and, 142–43

blinis, zucchini, 31

BLT roll-ups, 64

blueberry(ies):

in don't be blue (berries), 55

in fresh fruit and cheese martinis, 62

pancakes, 29

in Rachel's raspberry muffins variation, 39

in strawberry shortcake martinis variation, 225

bok choy, in Szechuan vegetable stir-fry, 152–53

bons bons, chocolate pecan, 215

bourbon barbecue sauce, no-cook, 89

grilled country-style pork ribs with, 120–21

bourbon maple glaze, baked ham with, 118–19

brandy, in Claire's stuffed pumpkin, 108–9

bread, pizza crust dough, 177

breading, for fried foods, 133

breakfast, 27–47

importance of, 27, 28

broccoli:

in kitchen sink quiche, 46–47

in mock fettuccine carbonara, 116–17

in vegetable soufflé variation, 159

brownies, chocolate pecan, with cream cheese frosting, 210–11

chicken (*cont.*)
  in vegetable egg foo yung variation,
    157
  wings, "if you had wings," 73
chiffonades, creating and cutting of, 177
chili:
  black soy bean, *see* black soy bean chili
  turkey burgers, 134–35
chili powder, in black soy bean chili,
    98–99
chili sauce, in cocktail sauce, 86
Chinese egg drop soup, 174
chips, crispy pepperoni, 54
chocolate:
  frosting, 232
  macadamia nut ice cream, 212–13
  pecan bons bons, 215
  pecan brownies with cream cheese
    frosting, 210–11
chocolate, unsweetened baking:
  in chocolate ganache, 214
  in chocolate pecan brownies with
    cream cheese frosting, 210–11
  in Stella Style chocolate chips, 209
chocolate chip muffins, 34–35
chocolate chips, Stella style, 209
  in cannoli parfaits, 230
chocolate ganache, 214
  in chocolate pecan bons bons, 215
  in don't be blue (berries), 55
chuck, ground:
  in black soy bean chili, 98–99
  in Gram's stuffed eggplant, 106–7
  in stuffed meat loaf rollatini, 102–3
cilantro:
  in black soy bean chili, 98–99
  in chicken with bacon, tomato, and
    thyme variation, 131
  in guacamole, 63

  in pico de gallo, 91
  vegetable kebabs, 192–93
cinnamon, roasted, candied nuts, Renee's,
    51
cioppino, seafood, 176–77
Claire's stuffed pumpkin, 108–9
clams:
  casino, 148–49
  in seafood cioppino, 176–77
club soda:
  in George's gorgeous macadamia
    banana muffins, 32
  in ham and Cheddar morning muffins,
    36–37
  in low-carb pizza, 58–59
  in Rachel's raspberry muffins, 38–39
  in spice muffins with cream cheese
    frosting, 40–41
  in zucchini muffins, 33
cocktail sauce, 86
cocoa powder, unsweetened:
  in chocolate frosting, 232
  in Neapolitan parfaits, 228–29
coconut, in refreshing fruit kcbabs, 56–57
cod, in seafood cioppino, 176–77
Colby cheese, in three-cheese veggie
    quesadillas, 154–55
Colby Jack Cheese:
  in Ginny's taco salad, 171
  in tequila chicken, 128–29
cole slaw, 196
  Waldorf, 195
collard greens, and roasted peppers, 194
Complete Low-Carb Home Chef
    Program, 12
condiments, 79–94
corned beef and cabbage, 100–101
country-style pork ribs, grilled, with
    bourbon barbecue sauce, 120–21

crab:
    snow, *see* snow crab
    -stuffed mushrooms, 68–69
crab cakes, Key West, with mustard sauce,
    146
cracked snow crab martinis, 147
cranberry, relish, 92
cream and strawberries parfait, 224
cream cheese:
    in chocolate pecan bons bons, 215
    in crab-stuffed mushrooms, 68–69
    in Key lime cheesecake, 218–19
    in pumpkin cheesecake, 220–21
    in Stella style New York ricotta
        cheesecake, 216–17
cream cheese frosting, 233
    chocolate pecan brownies with, 210–11
    spice muffins with, 40–41
cremini (Baby Bella) mushrooms:
    in turkey stroganoff, 138
    in wild mushroom ragout, 72
crêpes, 30
crispy pepperoni chips, 54
crust(s):
    pizza, baking of, 59
    pizza, bread, 177
    praline, for praline pumpkin pie,
        222–23
cucumber(s):
    in Ernie's Greek salad, 167
    in last-minute antipasto platter, 70–71
    in smoked salmon pinwheels, 65
    in Steph's sweet deli rolls, 53
    and tomato salad, 169
cumin, in black soy bean chili, 98–99

daiquiri, strawberry, 205
deep-fried onion rings, 188–89
deli rolls, Steph's sweet, 53

desserts, 207–33
dill:
    in chicken with bacon, tomato, and
        thyme variation, 131
    in grilled salmon with tomato herb
        relish, 140–41
    in old-fashioned egg mock potato salad
        variation, 187
don't be blue (berries), 55
Dr. Atkins New Diet Revolution (Atkins),
    8–9
dressing(s):
    Greek, 94
    quick raspberry vinaigrette, radicchio
        salad with, 170
    Thousand Island, 93

eating out, 22–23
egg(s):
    in blueberry pancakes, 29
    in chocolate pecan brownies with
        cream cheese frosting, 210–11
    in crêpes, 30
    foo yung, vegetable, 156–57
    in frittata Italiana, 42–43
    in George's gorgeous macadamia
        banana muffins, 32
    in ham and Cheddar morning muffins,
        36–37
    in Jimi's fried mozzarella sticks, 74–75
    in Key West crab cakes with mustard
        sauce, 146
    in kitchen sink quiche, 46–47
    in low-carb pizza, 58–59
    in Mamma Stella's stracciatella soup,
        174
    mock potato salad, old-fashioned, 187
    in on-hand omelet, 44–45
    in praline pumpkin pie, 222–23

iceberg lettuce:
    in BLT roll-ups, 64
    in ginger salad, 166
    in Ginny's taco salad, 171
    in minute steak salad, 168
ice cream, chocolate macadamia nut,
    212–13
"if you had wings" chicken wings, 73
Italian sausage:
    in frittata Italiana, 42–43
    in last-minute antipasto platter,
    70–71

jalapeño peppers:
    in pico de gallo, 91
    in tequila-marinated grilled boneless
    pork loin, 124–25
jicama matchstick fries, 190
Jimi's fried mozzarella sticks, 74–75

kebabs:
    cilantro vegetable, 192–93
    refreshing fruit, 56–57
ketchup, quick and easy, 82
Key lime cheesecake, 218–19
Key lime juice:
    in Key lime cheesecake, 218–19
    in Key West Caesar salad, 162–63
Key West Caesar salad, 162–63
Key West crab cakes with mustard sauce,
    146
kimchee, mussels, 150
King crab legs, in crab-stuffed
    mushrooms, 69
kitchen sink quiche, 46–47

lasagna, meat, 114–15
last-minute antipasto platter, 70–71
leeks, in ham and mock potato soup, 175

lemon juice, fresh:
    in sangria Stella style, 201
    in white wine spritzer, 200
lemon-lime:
    diet soda, in white wine spritzer, 200
    slushees, 203
lettuce, *see* iceberg lettuce; romaine
    lettuce; salad greens, mixed
lime juice, fresh:
    -lemon slushees, 203
    in mojito, 202
    in sangria, Stella style, 201
    in white wine spritzer, 200
lobster, in three-cheese veggie quesadillas
    variation, 155
Low Carb and Lovin' It, 12–13
Low-Carb Chefs, The, 12, 16
low-carb pizza, 58–59
Low-Carb Revolution, The, 12
low-fat foods, 17–18

macadamia nut(s):
    banana muffins, George's gorgeous,
    32
    chocolate ice cream, 212–13
    in nutty muddy trail mix variation, 52
mahi mahi, in seafood cioppino, 176–77
Mamma Stella's stracciatella soup, 174
maple bourbon glaze, baked ham with,
    118–19
martinis:
    cracked snow crab, 147
    fresh fruit and cheese, 62
    strawberry shortcake, 225
mayonnaise:
    in George's Gorgonzola salad, 164–65
    in Gorgonzola beef tenderloin
    variation, 113
    in horseradish cream sauce, 85

in mustard sauce, 83
in old-fashioned egg mock potato salad, 187
in remoulade sauce, 87
in sweet mustard sauce, 84
in Thousand Island dressing, 93
meat(s), 97–125
    lasagna, 114–15
    loaf rollatini, stuffed, 102–3
    see also specific meats
Mexican salad, 129
milkshake, strawberry, 204
mint:
    in mojito, 202
    for strawberry daiquiri, 205
minute steak salad, 168
mock fettuccine carbonara, 116–17
mock fried rice, shrimp, 145
mock potato(es):
    baked stuffed, 117
    egg salad, old-fashioned, 187
    garlic mashed, 181
    and ham soup, 175
mojito, 202
Monterey Jack cheese:
    in tequila chicken, 128–29
    in three-cheese veggie quesadillas, 154–55
mortadella, in last-minute antipasto platter, 70–71
mozzarella cheese:
    in bald calzone, 160
    in Gram's stuffed eggplant, 106–7
    in last-minute antipasto platter, 70–71
    in low-carb pizza, 58–59
    in meat lasagna, 114–15
    in minute steak salad, 168
    sticks, Jimi's fried, 74
    in stuffed meat loaf rollatini, 102–3

muffin(s):
    chocolate chip, 34–35
    cups, filling of, 32
    George's gorgeous macadamia banana, 32
    ham and Cheddar morning, 36–37
    Rachel's raspberry, 38–39
    spice, with cream cheese frosting, 40–41
    zucchini, *see* zucchini muffins
mushroom(s):
    button, *see* button mushrooms
    cleaning of, 69, 72
    crab-stuffed, 68–69
    enoki, in wild mushroom ragout, 72
    in kitchen sink quiche, 46–47
    oyster, in wild mushroom ragout, 72
    shiitake, *see* shiitake mushrooms
    straw, in Szechuan vegetable stir-fry, 152–53
    in stuffed meat loaf rollatini variation, 103
    wild, *see* wild mushrooms
mussels:
    debearding of, 150, 177
    kimchee, 150
    in seafood cioppino, 176–77
mustard sauce, 83
    Key West crab cakes with, 146
    sweet, 84

Neapolitan parfaits, 228–29
no-cook bourbon barbecue sauce, *see* bourbon barbecue sauce, no-cook
nuts:
    Renee's roasted cinnamon candied, 51
    see also specific nuts
nutty muddy trail mix, 52

salsa picante, in tequila chicken, 128–29

sangria, Stella Style, 201

satay, chicken, teriyaki ginger garlic,
76–77

sauces:
cocktail, 86
horseradish cream, 85
mustard, *see* mustard sauce
no-cook bourbon barbecue, *see*
bourbon barbecue sauce, no-cook
remoulade, 87

sausage:
and herb stuffing, 197
see also Italian sausage; pork breakfast
sausage

Sauvignon-Blanc, in white wine spritzer,
200

scallions, *see* green onions

scallops:
sea, *see* sea scallops
in Szechuan vegetable stir-fry variation,
153

scampi, Anaheim shrimp, 144

scampi butter, 88
in Anaheim shrimp scampi, 144
in seafood cioppino, 176–77
in wild mushroom ragout, 72

seafood, 139–50
cioppino, 176–77
see also specific seafood

sea scallops:
in Anaheim shrimp scampi variation,
144
blackened, with spinach and black soy
beans, 142–43
in seafood cioppino, 176–77

sesame, sesame seeds:
teriyaki tuna skewers, 66–67
toasting of, 67, 77

sherry, dry, in wild mushroom turkey
gravy, 80–81

shiitake mushrooms:
in wild mushroom ragout, 72
in wild mushroom turkey gravy, 80–81

shortcake, strawberry, martinis, 225

shrimp:
in blackened sea scallops with spinach
and black soy beans variation, 143
mock fried rice, 145
scampi, Anaheim, 144
in seafood cioppino, 176–77
in Szechuan vegetable stir-fry variation,
153
in vegetable egg foo yung variation, 157

slushees, lemon-lime, 203

smoked salmon pinwheels, 65

snacks, 49–59

snapper, in seafood cioppino, 176–77

snow crab:
cracked, martinis, 147
in seafood cioppino, 176–77

snow peas, in Szechuan vegetable stir-fry,
152–53

sopressata, in last-minute antipasto
platter, 70–71

soufflé, vegetable, 158–59

soup(s), 172–77
Chinese egg drop, 174
ham and mock potato, 175
Mamma Stella's stracciatella, 174
seafood cioppino, 176–77
turkey vegetable, 172–73

sour cream:
in Gorgonzola beef tenderloin
variation, 113
in guacamole, 63
in horseradish cream sauce, 85
in Key lime cheesecake, 218–19

veggie quesadillas, three-cheese, 154–55

vinaigrette, quick raspberry, radicchio salad with, 170

Waldorf cole slaw, 195

walnuts:

  in chocolate chip muffins as dessert, 35

  in George's gorgeous macadamia banana muffins variation, 32

  in George's Gorgonzola salad, 164–65

  in nutty muddy trail mix, 52

  in Renee's roasted cinnamon candied nuts, 51

  in Waldorf cole slaw, 195

whipped cream, Stella Style, 231

  in chocolate chip muffins as dessert, 35

  in strawberry shortcake martinis, 225

white wine spritzer, 200

wild mushroom:

  ragout, 72

  turkey gravy, 80–81

wine:

  red, in mussels kimchee, 150

  white, spritzer, 200

  see also specific wines

yellow squash:

  in cilantro vegetable kebabs, 192–93

  in Gram's stuffed eggplant variation, 107

  in grilled summer vegetables, 184–85

  in Szechuan vegetable stir-fry, 152–53

  in three-cheese veggie quesadillas, 154–55

  in vegetables casino, 182–83

  in vegetable soufflé, 158–59

  zucchini, and tomato fromage, 186

zucchini:

  blinis, 31

  in cilantro vegetable kebabs, 192–93

  in Gram's stuffed eggplant variation, 107

  in grilled summer vegetables, 184–85

  in kitchen sink quiche, 46–47

  in Szechuan vegetable stir-fry, 152–53

  in vegetable soufflé, 158–59

  yellow squash, and tomato fromage, 186

zucchini muffins, 33

  in sausage and herb stuffing, 197

  in strawberry shortcake martinis, 225